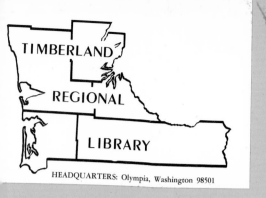

Tap Dancing

CONSTANCE ATWATER

Tap Dancing

TECHNIQUES, ROUTINES,

TERMINOLOGY

CHARLES E. TUTTLE COMPANY
Rutland, Vermont & Tokyo, Japan

Table of Contents

List of Illustrations

Introduction

WITH EVERY generation of children, approach and explanation in the teaching field must be revised and changed. As nations progress, and children are exposed to this advancement, their attitudes, abilities, and experiences differ greatly from those of their parents. Through television and travel, modern youth has a far greater knowledge of the artistic world than we had at their age. Their ability to grasp skills is sharp; their musical appreciation, due to television, movies, and records, is on a high plane; and their eagerness to learn and mimic is exceptional.

Because of this, along with any youth-work format, terminology and presentation must change to keep pace with the students. Most of the available information on tap dancing was written in the 1930s and this, like the school textbooks of that time, is certainly obsolete for today's young people. Although essentials remain the same, phrasing and explanation must be modernized with our present generation in mind.

Prior to this book, there has been very little material written about tap dancing. A few outdated pamphlets do exist, but a complete text on the subject, with thoroughly explained steps accompanied by pictures and sketches of footwork and technique, has simply not been available.

Tap Dancing: Techniques, Routines, and Terminology is an explanatory, technical, "how-to" text for the many students and teachers who will welcome it as a reference. It is also designed for the student who desires lessons, but for some reason does not have a teacher; the parent who wishes to gain greater knowledge in order to follow her child's progress; and the adult who has always longed to be able to tap dance, or who is engaged in some type of youth work where the ability to teach a few steps or routines would be advantageous.

Of course, it is impossible to make the learning of any art easy. One must apply oneself with interest and determination. One must read the directions carefully and follow each position and step slowly and patiently in the beginning. Practice and repetition bring forth familiarity and speed, and only through such repeated practice will one be able to progress from the basic, to the intermediate, to the advanced.

We all seem to be born with a definite appreciation of music, which can only be developed through the study of an art connected with music. Even toddlers grasp the feeling of rhythm as they take small steps in a circle when a catchy tune is played. There are very few individuals who can resist tapping the foot, clapping the hands, or keeping time in some manner to a rhythmic melody. Tap dancing is the only form of dance where one is following the exact beat of the music, and where one can definitely develop a sense of rhythm and timing. The quick footwork acquired through tap dancing enhances balance, coordination, and control.

The intricate knowledge and ability needed to become a good tap dancer lead the dance world. In ballet, a mood is created. Granted, one must develop slow, graceful movements and a strong body; however, the rhythmic control needed in tap dancing certainly does not enter into the ballet world. With modern dance, a lithe body and controlled movements are also needed, but again the stress is not placed on every beat of the music. When tap dancing, one is actually playing the number with one's feet. Each sound must be right on time, and the dancer must combine the smoothness of the muscian with the continuity of the arranger, and the animated movements of the conductor.

In recent years, the fundamentals of tap dancing have been neglected by some teachers and performers, who have instead attempted to combine this art with other forms of dance. I have watched students in Hawaiian skirts perform a combination tap dance-hula, which actually did nothing for the tap dance and left much to be desired for the hula. Another common sight is to see a child perform tap-dance steps along with combinations of ballet steps. This again leaves both forms of dance lacking in purpose and style in the presentation. In reality, tap dancing is such a satisfying form of expression that it is not necessary to combine it with any other form.

All countries have some form of dance that is immediately associated with that country or is, in a sense, considered the national dance. While the Irish are known for their jig, the Scottish for the highland fling, the Russians and French for their ballet, and the Slavic people for their polka, we Americans are known for our tap dancing.

With the founding of our country, a variety of dance forms arrived on our shores. It was with true American ingenuity that, from these various forms, a new and exciting means of expression was created and styled, completely different and refreshing. Thus tap dancing entered into the artistic world and gained considerable popularity. It has held its place as a favorite form of dance entertainment for many years.

This book has been written with the layman in mind. Thorough explanation of terminology is accompanied by illustrative pictures and sketches. An individual with no previous knowledge of tap dancing can follow the text and become a self-taught student. A child studying with a dance school will readily find references to any particular phase he or she might need help with between lessons. A teacher will discover new ideas and perhaps be refreshed on some forgotten bit of past knowledge, while a parent will be able to familiarize herself with tap-dancing terminology and assist her child in proper practice between classes.

The former teacher who wishes to refresh herself before starting classes again will find that there is much to be gained throughout this text. While on the other hand, the proprietor of a private kindergarten or nursery school, or the person starting a youth program, will discover routines suitable for their charges which are explained clearly enough for them to teach.

This book explains beginning fundamentals through intricate combinations; it progresses from handling the tiny tot to working with the teen-ager, and from costuming and routines to the finished production of the big recital. No phase has been overlooked or underemphasized.

Explanations of the various steps have been tested on beginning students to prove their clearness. Much of the terminology used in this book for combinations of steps eliminates the repetitious phrases used by teachers and students in schools of the past. This seems to make learning less difficult and in turn inspires greater interest and enthusiasm in the student.

1

Equipment and
Accessories

ONE DOES not need a great deal of equipment for tap dancing. A pair of tap shoes, with taps, and a comfortably fitting garment which allows freedom of movement are all that is absolutely essential. Other items which do assist the student are strictly optional.

The tap shoe, which is specially designed for long wear and comfortable fit, is usually in the five dollar price range and can be purchased at local shoe stores or through theatrical supply houses. The shoe is usually black patent leather, scientifically constructed for better balance. The student slipper has a one inch heel with a ribbon tie. However, a pair of taps on any well-fitting shoe will also serve the purpose.

I do not recommend heel plates for the beginner. The student must learn to rise to the tiptoe or ball of the foot and make a decided sound from the toe tap. If heel plates are used, it is very easy for the beginner to dance flat-footed and still get a tap sound. It is not the clear-ringing sound of the toe plate, but usually the student at first does not notice this difference. I also find that with both toe and heel plates the shoe is very slippery, and a child who is having difficulty with balance in the beginning stages will only have an added problem with heel plates.

There are numerous makes of toe plates and every teacher has her favorite. I prefer to start with a simple toe tap, eliminating washers and jingles, for these bring forth a false sound and do not allow the child to learn the proper basics.

Once into the advanced stage, a student will find the tap that suits his or her style.

The ribbon on the tap shoe can create problems. It is usually a black grosgrain ribbon and if tied properly will stay in place throughout the lesson or performance. However, many students hastily tie their ribbons and much class time is wasted while necessary stops are made in order for children to retie their shoes. Also, sometimes students appear in class without any ribbons in their tap shoes. Of course, this cannot be tolerated, for it is impossible to hop, shuffle, or kick with the toes curling under in order to hold the ribbon-less shoe in place. I find the best way to eliminate the ribbon-rascals is to absolutely insist, in the first few lessons, that all shoes are tied properly in a double bow before the student enters the classroom. If one finds this to be an impossibility with some of the younger children, a small, narrow strap may be purchased to replace the ribbon. This strap costs about fifty cents, and can be found at shoe repair shops or through theatrical supply stores.

To keep the inside of the shoe in good condition, a foot powder is essential. This not only prolongs the life of the shoe, but it makes it more comfortable and keeps it always fresh. I do allow my students to wear bobby socks with their tap shoes in class. This prevents blistering of the foot due to perspiration and rubbing. However, during a performance mesh tights or some type of stocking must be worn, for the bobby sock rarely adds to the beauty of a costume.

Tap shoes should be cared for as one cares for any special type of equipment. This means a periodic application of vaseline or patent cleaner. Ribbons should be washed and ironed occasionally and the shoe should be stored properly when not in use.

Many of my students stuff paper in the toes of their shoes, and keep them in a shoe box. Others have made themselves cloth carrying-cases for their shoes, which fit over heavy cardboard bottoms and have a drawstring top. Still others have the children's night cases which one can find in almost any department store. When a carrying case of any type is used, it is also possible to place the garment one wears in class in the case. The toe of the shoe should always be stuffed with tissue or paper to keep it from being flattened by some heavy object. Of course, a shoe tree can also be used, but many times after class the child will not take the time to insert the shoe tree, and in haste leave it behind in the dressing room.

There are many different types of garments which can be worn during tap-dancing lessons, and again each individual has her own preference. I prefer a seersucker, princess-line dress in colorful polka dots or pin stripes, with matching tights in a coordinating color. These tights may be sewn right into the dress, giving the student only one piece of wearing apparel to remember. Oftentimes when the tights are separate, the dressing room is full of forgotten tights after class.

The princess line in a dress allows freedom of movement, and the full skirt gives an attractive appearance when a dancer turns or performs quick changes of footwork. This garment is usually designed with a cap sleeve in the beginning, so that one is able to see all the arm placements, which are as important as the footwork. The seersucker material is easily laundered and does not require ironing. Other garments, such as shorts and a top, a circular skirt with top and tights, or any type of comfortably fitting summer sportswear may be used. I do not recommend slacks, capri pants, or long pants of any style for beginners, and the ballet leotard does not give the finished picture desired for the tap dancer.

A practice board can certainly be put to good use by the student, whether she is self-taught or enrolled in a school. This board can be made from a piece of plywood or any other type of wood. The length and width needed depend on the amount of space available for practice. The board should be cut in half, or even thirds, and hinged together. This makes it easy to move and requires little storage space when not in use.

One can readily see the purpose of a practice board. It is impossible to tap dance on carpeting and impractical to use waxed and polished floors of linoleum, tile, or hardwood in the home. This would create more work for parents and take the joy out of the child's progress. The cement on the patio or in the garage is not good for the taps and certainly not good for the shoes. A practice board can solve many of these problems of home practice or home instruction. If necessary, a piece of linoleum in the garage can be used as a substitute for a wooden practice board and functions equally as well.

Naturally, some type of music is required for tap dancing. Many schools engage piano players, while other instructors find the use of records or tapes most satisfactory. There are many companies that make records especially for tap-dancing students. These records have a slow pace on one side to use while learning, while on the flip side the entire number is played at the proper pace and can be used in the finished routine. The metronome count and the meter count are stated on the record, enabling the teacher or student to recognize the speed and the tempo of the number before purchasing the record. The length of playing time is also given.

For the self-taught student, records are most satisfactory. Not all of us are blessed with a piano and a friend or family member who would be able to play for us during practice. By using the specially designed tap-dancing records, a student is able to have the necessary music throughout the entire learning period and into the finished number. I have listed in the back of the book the names and addresses of companies where one can purchase records and other tap-dancing equipment.

At the dancing school, where one is working on highly polished floors, the rosin box plays an important part. By either sprinkling powdered rosin on the floor or having the students step into the rosin box before dancing, the danger of slipping is virtually eliminated. The self-taught student should also apply this safety precaution if she is working on polished or waxed floors. It is much easier to dance on a polished floor and the ring of the taps is clearer and more tinkling; however, if there is danger of slipping, the student automatically stiffens and the dancing is not relaxed.

A rosin box is filled with powdered rosin, which is inexpensive and lasts for quite a long time. If there is not enough room for a box, the rosin can be kept in the bag it comes in when purchased, and sprinkled over the floor before class or practice. It is also wise for a dancer to take a small bag of rosin with her to a performance. Oftentimes, floors and stages are highly polished and dangerously slick.

Another very old method of eliminating slipperiness is with the watering can. This method was used prior to the advent of rosin and is still applied in some schools. A typical sprinkling can with small holes which produce a fine spray is suitable; floors are sprinkled prior to a class, practice, or performance.

It is easy to understand why safety measures should be used in regard to slippery floors. Not only is it embarrassing to fall during a class or performance, but it could also result in injury. In the beginning, a student is having enough difficulty with balance without adding other elements to this.

If one is working with groups of students, a large room is the most comfortable place to practice. With space to move around in, the student feels freer and can use smoother motions when dancing. However, if it is impossible to obtain a large room, the instructor can utilize the space available by staggering the lines or arranging the students in a "V" or "T" manner; this gives each individual more freedom than the straight-line placement. Also, in small areas the students should be allowed to practice turns and jumps individually as well as in a group, in order to enhance the feeling of space and freedom.

Once the students are over the beginning phases, a mirror in the classroom or practice area is very valuable. This makes it possible for the student to correct body posture, perfect arm placements, and develop a feeling of confidence by being able to see the overall appearance of very step. The habits and techniques which are gained through practice stay with a dancer during a performance. It is therefore most important that each developed habit is a good one; each technique is properly performed; and each individual posture adds to a refreshing presentation. The mirror makes all of this possible.

Although teachers follow a similar format in class scheduling, no two individuals teach exactly alike. One teacher often stresses one particular phase or technique, while another favors an altogether different method or area. This is only natural, for none of us is a duplicate of another. All of us have different thought processes, theories, and approaches, as well as different presentations. The personality of the teacher plays a significant role in the development of a student. A particular student might do extremely well under the guidance of one teacher but show little advancement when placed with another teacher. This does not mean that the first teacher was superior in her knowledge, but it does mean that, because of her personality and approach, she was better able to reach that particular child. The second teacher would probably be equally effective with other students responsive to her methods and approach.

Dancing teachers are usually very understanding individuals, who have the student's progress in dancing foremost in their minds. No teacher is resentful when a student changes to another studio or school, if the student will benefit in making such a change. In fact, the majority of teachers will suggest change if they are not satisfied with the progress of a student and feel a different teacher could contribute more to the student's advancement.

It is also humanly impossible for two persons to dance exactly alike. Granted, in precision lines such as the Rockettes, every movement seems to be completely unified. However, each person's individual attitude toward the music and the choreography is different, and although movements are precise, expressions and feelings vary greatly. In time, every dancer develops what is known as her own individual style. You cannot expect a tall person to perform dance steps and body movements in the same manner as a shorter person. The long-limbed student will no doubt be able to execute higher kicks and brilliant leg rolls, while the shorter-limbed student, who does not have the added height and leg length, will excel in wings and hassocks. Because of such individual traits and abilities, no two students should ever be compared by a teacher, parent, or classmate.

As one progresses in tap dancing, one soon discovers that advanced and intermediate steps are often combinations of basic movements using different foot placements, different accents on the tap, different timing, and perhaps added hops or shuffles. As these combinations were developed and passed down from teachers to students, some were named and some were not. I have found through my many years of teaching that the named combinations, once we have gone through the process of breakdown while learning, are readily remembered by my students. This eliminates having to repeat the phrasing of the footwork as the class does the step. I merely mention the name of the combination and immediately the class associates the name with the correct footwork.

In the past few years of teaching, I have given every combination a name and have found that this often speeds progress and can be a definite asset when designing routines. By merely telling the students the names of the various combinations which are included in the choreography of the routine, much time is saved and the routine is grasped more quickly by the class. All of our original combinations are immediately named and the students' class notebooks contain each named combination followed by a detailed breakdown as it has been taught in class. This eliminates any possibility of forgetting or misunderstanding. Even though combinations have been practiced separately before routines are set, however, it is still necessary to spend a great deal of time practicing the routine itself. The beat of the music, stage placement, and accentuation vary with each number and the only way to polish these to perfection is through concentrated practice.

You will find through this text, after the beginning basics, that every combination has its own name. You must remember the name as you practice the footwork, for the routines at the end of each chapter will have only the name of the combination and the number of times it is executed. You will also find that after practice your mind quickly associates the name with the footwork; thus, the mind controls the body, as you automatically go through the footwork of the combination.

Along with the combinations, there are also special steps to remember. These tap steps are also named and it would be wise to jot them down in your class notebook, too, to have on hand to refresh your memory.

As you progress in the study of tap dancing, you will realize that it is a very fascinating form of expression. You will also benefit from the mental stimulation, the healthful exercise, and the poise and confidence you will gain through your knowledge and ability to perform an exhibitive art. You will develop good posture, a graceful and rhythmic walk, an appreciation of music, and the understanding of a technical and intricate skill. Along with all of this, you will feel the pride and satisfaction which comes from involving your energies in a form of self-improvement.

2
Beginning Fundamentals

IN THE BEGINNING, tap-dancing terminology varies somewhat with every teacher and sometimes even with every class. I find that I use different phrasing with each beginners' class. While some students can grasp a "brush-brush, step" term quickly, others cannot, and it is therefore necessary to use another phrase. I may say "front, back, down" for some classes, which describes what the foot is actually doing, or I may explain the footwork and simply count "one, two, three" to bring about quick results. I rarely use the old-fashioned term "ball change" in my tap-dancing instruction. I find that it is not easily understood by my beginning students, and that other phrases are more effective and eliminate confusion.

One learns through experience exactly what phrasing is best for each class; I often use a combination of words to put timing and step motions across to some students. For example, "What's the time?" in place of "brush-brush, step" sometimes works well with some groups. The important factor is not the wording of the instructions, however, but the fact that the student is grasping the foot motion. Proper terminology should be learned, but this comes with time and is not usually expected in the very first few lessons.

The most important element in learning any skill is mastering the preliminary basics that enable one to progress to other phases with less difficulty and greater understanding. Through tap-dancing basics, the student learns to control her balance, to move right foot and left foot, to shift weight quickly, and to keep exact time to the music. She also learns to rise to the balls of the feet for each tap sound and this, although it may sound simple, is quite difficult to conquer.

In the very first class, one must strongly emphasize that a dancer does not watch her feet. Eyes should be focused on the teacher or be looking straight ahead; the feet will move properly without being watched. If a teacher allows a student to develop this habit when learning, it may take months to correct. When a student progresses to the point of routines, she simply cannot perform and satisfy an audience with her head tilted down and her eyes following each foot motion.

Class or practice period should always start with warm-up exercises. These help to make the body limber and also to tone the muscles. Exercises should not be overdone in the beginning, however, so the first few are simple in design yet have a definite purpose.

TOE SLAPS

The first exercise should be Toe Slaps. These are done slowly when introduced, for the student will find it difficult to hold the ball of the foot position in the beginning.

1. Place both hands on the hips to aid in balance and rise to the balls of the feet.

2. Standing in place, slap right, left, right, left in a forward motion.

You should be thinking: slap step (right), slap step (left). As balance develops, this can be done to a very quick melody.

RELAX BEND EXERCISE

Next we relax the body with a Relax Bend Exercise. This is very helpful in relieving the tensions which naturally tighten muscles.

1. Standing with feet together, place both arms high over your head.

2. Start shaking your arms and lowering them slowly in front of your body.

3. Allow your shoulders to slowly droop, moving them up and down in a relaxed motion.

4. Slowly bend from the waist, keeping your knees stiff and keeping your arms and shoulders moving slightly up and down, completely relaxed.

5. Bend forward slowly and place your palms flat on the floor in front of your toes. Remember your knees should be straight.

6. Hold this position for a second and then slowly raise your arms to the overhead position and repeat the exercise.

You might find at first that it is impossible for you to touch the floor without bending your knees. Should this be the case, push your palms as far as you can keeping the knees straight. In a very short time, your muscles will become limber and your palms will touch flat on the floor as you maintain the locked knee position.

KNEE-TO-CHEST EXERCISE

Students will also benefit greatly from the Knee-to-Chest Exercise. This, too, will require some time before the knee rises in the chest height position while proper posture is being maintained.

1. Stand tall, with your shoulders back and hands on hips.

2. Raise your right leg with toe down, knee bent as high as you can without letting your shoulders pull forward.

3. Simultaneously, keeping your left leg locked, hop on the ball of your left foot.

4. Return your right leg to the floor and repeat the exercise with the left leg.

Be sure that you do not give in to the tendency of letting your shoulders fall forward. They must be pulled back and the leg that remains on the floor should not bend while you are doing the hop.

ARM AND WRIST RELAXATION

The arms, which play a very important part in tap dancing, must be limber, and it is wise to go through an arm exercise at the beginning of class.

1. Drop your arms to the sides of your body.

2. Allow your shoulders to droop slightly.

3. Slowly shake your arms and wrists, letting your shoulders move up and down with the motion.

This exercise is not done with speed but at a very slow pace, allowing the movement to slowly relax arm muscles and limber the wrists.

Proper and graceful arm placements add the finishing touch to a tap dancer. Many times the arm placements are designed to assist in balance, while other times they are created to add grace and flair to the body and the footwork. Regardless of their purpose, however, a dancer who is not taught in the beginning to use different arm placements will never have the appearance of a polished performer. One must start the beginner off with arm placements as well as foot placements, for by so doing arm placements become automatic and are never awkward or overexaggerated.

When working with my beginner students, each basic step has a specific arm placement. These are learned along with the footwork, and oftentimes it is possible to guide students through an entire dance, once steps are learned, by merely demonstrating the arm placements. The illustrated arm and hand movements are quickly associated mentally with the corresponding footwork. Of course, as students progress, arm placements change; however, the beginner must be instructed to follow the arm placements as well as the footwork.

Through all the basic steps in the following pages, the arm placement is described along with the step itself. As you practice arm placements, you will find that when you go into the set routines at the end of the chapters, you will have no trouble using your arms. By so doing, you add the finishing touch to your number.

Since the right foot and left foot must be readily distinguished by the student, the beginning basic steps stress changing from right to left and shifting weight quickly. Maintaining balance and keeping a steady, rhythmic count are also emphasized.

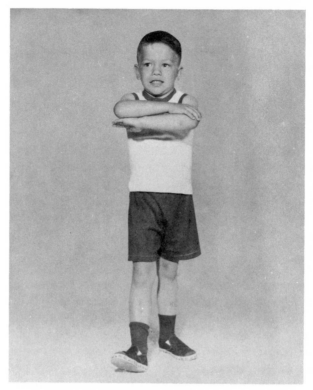

1. Heel Drops, Step 1.

HEEL DROPS

Place your arms in front of your body at chest height, with elbows bent. The right arm should lie on top of the left arm, with your right fingers near your left elbow. Feet are placed side by side.

1. Move your right heel a few inches to the front, with the toe up off the floor (Fig. 1).

2. Step back on your right foot, placing it next to your left foot, and shift all your weight to your right foot on the step.

3. Repeat the movements with your left foot.

You should be thinking: heel, step; heel, step, or counting 1–2, 3–4.

DIGS

Bend your elbows at waist height, with both arms at the side of your body. Your right arm should extend to the right and your left arm to the left, with hands posed gracefully. Your feet are placed side by side, with weight on the left foot.

1. Cross your right foot in a toe-down position in front of and to the left of the left ankle (Fig. 2).

2. Tap your right toe on the floor.

3. Return your right foot to the starting position, and shift your weight to the right.

4. Repeat with your left foot.

You should be thinking: cross, tap, step; cross, tap, step as each foot goes through its proper motion.

JUMPS

Beginner Jumps are very simple to execute but to do them properly, you must learn to land quietly and gracefully with arms in a natural position.

Start with your hands on your hips. As you execute the Jump, your hands come off your hips and move in at waist height, then rise up over your head, with the right arm going to the right and the left arm to the left. The design is finished with each arm making a circle and returning back to the hips.

1. Your weight should be evenly distributed on both feet.

2. Bend your knees slightly and push with your feet, thus sending your body off the floor and into the air momentarily.

3. Keep your toes pointed downward while your body is in the air.

4. End the jump by landing on the floor quietly, with slightly bent knees.

When doing the Jump, you will land very flat-footed in the beginning, with your heels and toes touching the floor at the same time. However, with practice you will soon learn to land on the balls of your feet. In the beginning, you will land very heavily, too, for it takes time to develop enough coordination to sink slightly into a knee bend as you hit the floor, thereby breaking the force of the landing.

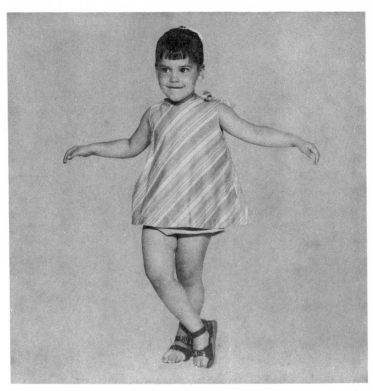

2. Digs, Step 1.

It would be wise now to do a series of these first basic steps to music, remembering to go from one arm placement into the other as you change footwork. I would suggest you use "Swanee River" as your music and perform each complete basic step eight times before changing. Each completed step will be given a one count. For example, for Heel Drops you will do right foot heel, step and count that as one. When you repeat the heel, step with your left foot, that counts as two; thus each change of feet will be one count, which will enable you to keep track of eight counts and keep up with your music. Each completed Jump will receive one count, although you might be thinking up, down through the execution.

For those of you who do not understand measure, I will simplify this by further explanation. Most of you know the words to this old favorite, so the following should help you to recognize your count:

> *Way*—right Heel Drop
> *down upon*—left Heel Drop
> *the Swanee*—right Heel Drop
> *River*—left Heel Drop
> *Far*—right Heel Drop
> *far*—left Heel Drop
> *awa*—right Heel Drop
> *aay*—left Heel Drop.

By following this timing, you can change from Heel Drops, to Digs, to Jumps, and back to Heel Drops. Remember you must keep time with the music and use your arm placements as well as the proper footwork. After practicing this a few times, you will remember your arm placements easily, and be able to change your footwork in time to the music. When you have reached this point, you should change from eight complete executions of each step to four, and speed up your arm placements and footwork. This will necessitate faster changes of weight and help develop better balance.

The next two basics are designed to teach forward and backward movement with proper balance and timing.

SIMPLE STRUT

Your arms are placed at the sides of the body and more or less follow the foot movements. As the right foot moves forward, your right arm swings forward, too. However, this is not a high swing, for the arm is actually just a little above waist height in its highest position through the movement. As your left foot starts forward, your left arm also moves forward, and the right arm comes back to its original position at the side of the body (Fig. 3).

1. With the right toe leading, your right foot stretches forward, and the toe taps on the floor. Your weight is on the left foot, and as the heel of your right foot hits the floor, your weight shifts to the right foot.

3. Simple Strut.

2. Your left foot, which is now about six inches behind the right foot, moves forward with the toe leading, and the same procedure is executed with the left foot.

You should be thinking: toe, heel; toe, heel as you move forward with the strutting motion.

SCOOT BACKS

This step will teach the student to move backward and, because clapping is used to accompany the movements, it will also assist the student in keeping time with the beat of the music.

1. Your weight should be distributed evenly on both feet.

4. Scoot Backs, Step 2.

2. Bend your knees slightly, keeping your shoulders back; do not lean forward (Fig. 4).

3. Make a slight jump backward, (Fig. 5) really more of a scoot since you do not move very high off the floor. Straighten your knees as you rise to the balls of both feet.

4. Sink into the bent-knee position and repeat the step.

5. Clap your hands as your knees straighten when you move backward.

As with the Jump, you will find yourself landing on the flat of each foot instead of the balls of the feet in the beginning, but this can be quickly corrected with a little practice.

In order to combine a backward and forward movement

32 TAP DANCING

5.   Scoot Backs, Step 3.

and keep your balance, you should practice these last two steps a few times without music until you feel sure of your hand and foot placement. I suggest that you do eight Simple Struts forward, again counting one for each complete execution. Then do eight Scoot Backs backward, remembering the count by the clap of your hands. As soon as the movements no longer feel foreign to you, play the "Swanee River" record again and do four Simple Struts forward and four Scoot Backs. Repeat this until you are using relaxed arm movements, staying on the balls of your feet, and are confident of your footwork. Be sure to stay with your music. In time you will find that you have developed an accurate sense of keeping time to music.

Pull Backs could really be classified as an exercise. However, in my classes we find it more enjoyable to use them as a basic step and utilize them in beginner dance-routines. They are designed to assist with leg control and to coordinate arm motions with footwork.

Your arms should be placed at the sides of the body, and will follow the same motion that the feet and legs are using.

1. Stand with your feet side by side. Shift weight to the left foot.

2. Extend your right foot and leg about 12 inches to the front.

3. Bend your left leg, keeping your right leg straight, with your weight still on the left foot.

4. Stomp your right foot on the floor and pull it straight back to the starting position beside the left foot, as the left leg straightens.

5. Quickly shift your weight to the right foot, bend the right knee, and repeat the step with your left foot.

You should be thinking: stomp, pull when performing this step. The same arm as the moving foot stretches to the front on the stomp, with fingers extending close to the knee of the outstretched leg. As you can see, it takes a deep knee bend on the other foot to place the fingers in this position. When the leg pulls back, the arm also pulls back, with the hand moving to near hip position.

While doing Pull Backs you must learn to shift weight quickly and to simultaneously bend the knee of one leg while executing the stomp with the opposite foot. Although this sounds very simple, you will find that it takes time to coordinate all of the footwork and arm movements.

BEGINNING BRUSH-BRUSH STEP

The Shuffle, or Brush-Brush, Step, is used constantly in tap dancing and we start learning it in the very beginning phase. There are numerous breakdowns for this. I have found the following to be the most successful.

1. Place your hands on your hips to assist balance. Your feet are side by side with weight on the left foot.

2. Using only the toe of the right foot for sound, execute a small kick forward. This is called a brush.

3. Using only the toe of the right foot again execute a small kick backward, which brings the foot back to its original starting position, near the right side of the left ankle.

4. Step down on the right foot and immediately shift weight to the right foot as you brush the left foot forward off the floor and backward to the starting position.

I find the phrasing "front, back, down, change feet" is quite successful in establishing this footwork in the minds of my beginners. The student who is concentrating very hard on foot placement oftentimes will not remember to shift weight and change to the other foot unless reminded. Also the phrasing describes what the feet are doing and this helps considerably. Once the footwork has been learned it is not difficult to change the phrasing from "front, back, down," to "brush-brush, step," and after practice the student remembers, completely on her own, to change from the right to left foot after a completed execution.

Another phrase I have found helpful in some classes when teaching fundamentals of the shuffle is "What's the time?" I use this with many classes when trying to develop more speed in the execution and still keep the timing. We add a bit of a singsong to the phrase and it does help in developing a continuity of rhythm for the Brush-Brush, Step. You will readily recognize placement through the phrasing: What's (brush) the (brush) time (step)?

To progress with the beginning Shuffle, add the basic Jump explained previously. Use the same arm movement learned for the Jump.

1. Execute one Jump, returning your hands to your hips, with weight on both feet.

2. Shifting your weight to the left foot, execute a Brush-Brush, Step with the right foot.

3. Shifting weight to the right foot, execute a Brush-Brush, Step with the left foot.

You should be thinking: jump, front, back, down; jump, front, back, down; or jump, brush-brush, step; jump, brush-brush, step; or jump, what's the time; jump, what's the time,

6. Toe Points, Step 2.

depending on which phrasing suits you the best. This routine
is excellent training and in time will lead to the Hop, Shuffle,
Step, or what is commonly referred to as Threes or Triples.

TOE POINTS

Toe points can be used in many ways and in many directions. To help the student realize different floor placements
and to add variety to the first few lessons, these are introduced with the footwork going toward the back.

1. Place your feet side by side, with weight on the left foot.

2. Move your right foot in a toe-down position behind
and about four inches to the left of the left foot (Fig. 6).
The very tip of the tap touches the floor.

3. Return your right foot to its starting position, and shift weight to the right foot.

4. Repeat with the left foot, starting with Step 2.

Your arms are held in the same position to start as in Digs; as you point your right toe behind the left leg, lean your body to the right, causing your right arm to drop down with the hand near knee height. Your left arm is raised high with the elbow near head height. Alternate this arm motion as you execute the Toe Point with the left foot. You might think: toe, step; toe, step while doing Toe Points.

After practicing the above step until your arm placement and footwork are coordinated, you will enjoy trying a variation. This is a series of Toe Points done in a circle. Do a Toe Point in exactly the same manner as described previously while turning your body to the left with each step. At first use eight Toe Points to complete your circle. As soon as you are able to do the footwork, arm placements, and body turns without studied concentration, cut the number to four Toe Points.

CROSS TURN

Turns in tap dancing are very effective and add much style to a routine. It is important that the beginner is introduced to turns during the early stages of learning, in order to develop grace and balance while changing body positions. A very basic turn which is almost self-explanatory is the Cross Turn.

1. Cross your right foot in front of the left foot very close to the ankle. Your weight should be on both feet (Fig. 7).

2. Do not start turning your body until the above foot position is completed.

3. Rise high on the half toe (tip of toes) and with a push of your shoulders toward the left, your body starts a turn to the left, which completes a full circle in two stages.

4. *Do not move your feet by taking small steps during the turn.*

5. As your body completes a half-turn, your back is toward what would be the audience (Fig. 8), the crossed position in which you started opens up, and your feet are together again side by side.

 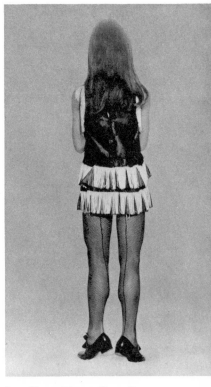

7. Cross Turn, Step 1.   8. Cross Turn, Step 5.

6. As you continue turning to the left to complete the circle, your left foot crosses in front of the right foot near the ankle (Fig. 9).

7. Drop from the half-toe position so that your feet are flat on the floor. You are now back in a crossed position but *with the left foot in front*.

8. Move your right foot from behind the left foot, extend it to the right as your left knee bends out over your left toe, and with the toe of your right foot hit the floor three times with the tap of the shoe.

You should be thinking: cross and turn and tap, tap, tap. You must remember to cross your feet near the ankles, rise high on the half toe, and keep your legs locked throughout

9. Cross Turn, Step 6.

the spinning turn. The shoulder push should not be over-exaggerated, but done with just enough force to start the body in its circle.

In the Cross Turn, arms are at waist height, elbows bent, with hands posed nicely. The right hand should extend to the right and the left hand to the left. On the turn, the hands gracefully move into a position in front of the body at waist height; elbows are rounded and the hands are posed closer together. On the tap, tap, tap the right arm extends to the right with the hand down below knee position. The left arm is held in a diagonal position away from the body and extending to a position above the head.

BEGINNING FUNDAMENTALS   39

LUNGE

A Lunge is a momentary pause where one must hold an exact body position, and also maintain perfect balance. There are many variations of Lunges, with new ones being originated all the time. The beginner starts with a very simple Lunge, for holding proper balance and position during the length of the pause will take some time to achieve.

1. Place feet side by side with weight distributed evenly.

2. Spring forward, landing on your right foot with knee bent, shoulders back, and body straight.

3. At the same time, extend your left leg in the air behind the body. The leg should be in a locked position, with foot arched and toe pointing to the back.

During the Lunge, the right arm is held at an angle diagonal from the body to the front, with the hand posed gracefully above the head. The left arm extends to the back in a position similar to that of the left leg, but at waist height. You must learn to hold a Lunge while maintaining proper posture, arm placement, and balance. An excellent way to practice Lunges is from the Cross Turn. Immediately after the tap, tap, tap, go into a Lunge and hold it for two counts.

When practicing Lunges, it is wise to reverse foot positions and do the Lunge on the left foot as well as the right. Most people, being right-handed, have a tendency to favor right footwork and right arm movements. The left foot, leg, and arm must also be developed, however, and every step or combination should be repeated with the left leg and arm following the action of the right leg and arm.

After repeated practice of the Lunge and the other previous steps, you should notice a significant improvement in your balance and coordination. Your arms are no longer moving awkwardly, and you can quickly shift your weight from one foot to the other without losing your balance or the beat of the music. When you reach this point, you are ready for some more advanced steps.

HOP BRUSH-BRUSH STEP

This step, also known as Threes or Triples, is done by eliminating the jump on both feet and doing a jump on one

Hop right.	*Brush.*	*Brush.*	*Step left.*

10.   Hop Brush-Brush Step, Step 5.

foot. Hands are placed on the hips to aid in good balance.

1. Shift weight to your left foot.

2. Hop on the left foot, a small hop, as you raise your right foot off the floor.

3. Brush-brush, step with your right foot.

4. As you step down on your right foot, put all your weight on that foot and raise your left foot off the floor.

5. Hop on the right foot and brush-brush, step with your left foot, simultaneously raising your right foot as the left foot does the step and receives your weight (Fig. 10).

You should be thinking: hop, brush-brush, step; hop, brush-brush, step, for you have practiced to a point where you no longer need the explanatory phrasing we used in the beginning breakdown of the Shuffle.

Be sure to quickly shift weight on the step and make your hop on the foot which has just finished the step. You change from right foot to left foot with each hop. As your proficiency develops you can substitute the word shuffle for brush-brush, and the step can then be thought of as hop, shuffle, step; hop, shuffle, step.

With a little effort, the preceding basics can be learned

quickly and easily. In order for you to feel a greater sense of accomplishment, however, I have utilized these steps in setting up two very easy-to-follow routines. I find that it is far more enjoyable to practice the basics of tap dancing if they are incorporated in dance form. Dances designed for the beginner, using simple steps, can be quite original and even performed for your classmates, neighbors, or friends.

Since you have already used the "Swanee River" melody for combination practice, it will be used again in the following routines. You have familiarized yourself with the rhythm, so it will be much easier for you keep up with the music as you proceed with your first dance.

DANCE NUMBER FOR BEGINNERS

ROUTINE: "Swanee River" (Russell record)
     4/4 meter time, met beat 126
     3 chord, 4-bar introduction
     2 choruses
     48 bars

Since your knowledge at the moment is still limited, most basic steps are done a total of four times before changing steps. This will call for repetition of some of the basics throughout the routine. Again, the words are used for the benefit of those who are still having trouble with count and do not understand the musical terminology of measures and bars. In keeping with the easy theme, every change of basics is started on the right foot. Arm placements are not listed, for by now the mention of a step should automatically bring to mind the appropriate arm movements.

1. On introduction (three chords and four bars), immediately after the third cord, start from the right of the stage and enter to center stage doing a total of eight Simple Struts. The first six of these are done with the right side to the audience (r.l.r.l.r.l.). On the last two Simple Struts, turn and face the audience (r.l.).

2. Jumps: four times (*Way* 1, *down upon* 2, *the Swanee* 3, *River* 4).

3. Digs: four times (*far* 1, *far* 2, *awa-* 3, *-ay* 4).

4. Brush-Brush, Step, change feet: four times (*There's where my heart* 1, *is yearning ever* 2, *there's where the old* 3, *folks stay* 4).

5. Toe Points, making a circle to the left: four times (*All up and* 1, *down the* 2, *whole crea-* 3, *-tion* 4).

6. Simple Struts, forward: four times (*Sad-* 1, *-ly I* 2, *roa-* 3, *-mm* 4).

7. Cross Turn and tap, tap, tap, tap: one time (*Still longing for*—Cross Turn, *the old plantation*—tap, tap, tap, tap).

8. Lunge forward on the right foot and hold (*and for the*).

9. Step down on the left foot, bringing the right leg up near the left knee in a toe-down position with weight on the left foot (*old folks*).

10. Repeat Lunge on the right, stepping on the left with feet side by side (*at home*).

This is the end of the first chorus. You should sense your timing now, so it will not be necessary to repeat the words through the rest of the routine.

11. Jump, Brush-Brush, Step: four times.

12. Scoot Backs: four times.

13. Pull Backs: four times.

14. Brush-Brush, Step, change: four times.

15. Heel Drops: four times.

16. Cross Turn and tap, tap, tap, tap: one time.

17. Quickly turn to the right of the stage with your left side to the audience. Starting on the right foot, do four Simple Struts to the right of the stage.

18. Still with your left side to the audience, do Toe Points to the back, in place: four times.

19. Still with left side to the audience, do Scoot Backs: four times.

20. Do four Heel Drops. The first two (r.l.) are with your left side to the audience and the next two (r.l.) facing the audience.

21. Brush-Brush, Step, change: four times.

22. Digs: four times.

23. Cross Turn and Lunge for bow.

ROUTINE: "Swanee River"

SONG:

> *Say, did you know that we are dancers,*
> *though we are small!*
> *Teacher says that we're her star prancers,*
> *the very best of them all!*

Right foot (raise right foot with toe down and touch knee with right hand).

Left foot (repeat same leg and arm action).

Toe Point, Toe Point (do the point with the right foot and then with the left).

Slowly cross and turn (do Cross Turn while singing).

Heel Drop, Heel Drop (do Heel Drop, first right and then left, while singing).

Strut 1, Strut 2 (do Simple Struts while singing).

This is what we learn (hands on hips and bend both knees).

DANCE:

Jumps: four times.
Toe Points in circles: four times.
Brush-Brush, Step, change: four times.
Digs: two times.
Heel Drops: two times.
Struts, forward: four times.
Scoot Backs: four times.
Struts, forward: two times.
Cross and turn: one time.

SONG again:

> *Now, don't you see that we are dancers,*
> *though we are small?*
> *Don't you agree that we're star prancers,*
> *the very best of them all!*

Right foot, left foot, Toe Point, Toe Point.
Slowly cross and turn.
Heel Drop, Heel Drop, Strut 1, Strut 2.
This is what we learn.
(The song is again accompanied by the indicated
motions, and ended with a curtsey.)

These two very simple routines utilizing the basic movements add more interest to your practice periods, for the
melody will develop a feeling of continuity and rhythm. The
fact that you are doing a simple dance routine will give you
a sense of progress and will increase your desire to learn.

3

Pre-intermediate Fundamentals

NOW THAT you have progressed through the beginning basics you should find that you are much better coordinated, balance is easier to keep, and weight changes from the right to left foot are no longer a problem.

Although you still have a long way to go before completely understanding the art of tap dancing, you are now ready for more difficult steps that will call for more adroit movements. You will find that tap dancing, like any other art, is most difficult for you in the beginning stage. But once you become familiar with the needed techniques, terminology, and arm and foot placements, even though steps become harder, you are more agile and have less trouble executing the placements. In order to keep the agility you are now developing it is necessary to add more exercises to the agenda.

CIRCULAR BENDS

Circular Bends not only help to make you limber, they also help you to keep a trim waistline and a firm abdomen.

1. Arms are stretched high over the head. Stand with feet side by side, very tall, legs stiff.

2. Bend your body from the waist to the right, both arms now stretching out in a horizontal position to the right.

3. Still bending from the waist, swing your arms from the right, down, and in front of the body.

4. The knees stay stiff as the fingertips of each hand touch

the toes. The hands pass to a horizontal position to the left and back up over the head.

Your arms make a circular motion from high over your head, to the right, over the toes, to the left, and back over your head. Do not bend the knees as the fingertips pass over the toes, keep both legs straight.

PENDULUM KICKS

In order to do this exercise it will be neccessary to hold onto the back of a chair or table that reaches near waist height. In the beginning you need a stationary object to enable you to maintain your balance through Pendulum Kicks. For explanation purposes the left leg is used as the kicking leg. However, this must be done with both legs.

1. The right hand is placed on a waist-high chair or table. Feet are together. Stand tall with tummy in and shoulders pulled back. Throughout this exercise the upper part of the body stays very stiff and you move from the hips down only.

2. As you swing your left leg forward and off the floor, spring to the half toe on your right foot, keeping the knees of both legs locked.

3. As you swing your left leg back in a locked position, your right foot takes a small hop and lands in a flat position on the floor.

4. Repeat this action swinging the right leg front and back.

Your leg should be moving just like the pendulum of a clock. You must remember to keep your shoulders pulled back and not lean your body forward and backward with the leg motion. Once you have practiced this for a period of time you will find that it is not necessary to grasp a stationary object for you will have perfected your ability to keep your balance.

As new exercises are introduced you must not neglect your previously learned ones. This, of course, is also true with the fundamentals and basic steps. It is always wise to spend some of your practice time or lesson time doing review work.

After successfully conquering the Hop, Shuffle, Step, which is sometimes called Threes, you are ready to experiment more with Shuffles. A Shuffle is a front brush followed by a back brush, which can be executed to the front, side, or back. By adding a step after a Shuffle, you find that with proper accent you can do the basic Irish Jig Step.

IRISH JIG STEPS

1. Place your hands on your hips. As you perform with your right foot, the right shoulder swings forward. This motion is repeated using the left shoulder as you do the step with your left foot.

2. Weight is on the left foot. Keeping your foot very close to the floor, do a Brush-Brush, Step with the right foot.

3. On the step, your weight is shifted to the right foot, and your left foot then does a Brush-Brush, Step.

4. The accent is on the step, with the brush-brush of the tap being softer than the step.

You should be thinking: brush-brush, *step;* brush-brush, *step;* or, perhaps, one two, *three;* one two, *three.* In order to feel the rhythm of the step, the tune "Irish Washerwoman" is ideal for practice. This record can be obtained as a student practice record, or perhaps you can just hum the melody as you do the step.

IRISH JIG HOPS

This is a combination which we call Irish Jig Hops, and you will enjoy learning this step to go along with the above jig.

1. Hop on the left foot, extend your right foot about four inches to the front and place the heel of your right foot on the floor (Fig. 11).

2. Hop on the left foot, bring your right foot back near starting position, and tap the toe on the floor (Fig. 12).

3. Hop on the left foot, raising your right foot off the floor again (Fig. 13).

4. Step on your right foot, shifting weight to this foot.

5. Step on your left foot, shifting weight to this foot.

6. Step again on your right foot, shifting weight to this foot, and repeat starting with Step 1, using the right foot for the hop and the left foot for the movement.

11. Irish Jig Hops, Step 1.   12. Irish Jig Hops, Step 2.

Steps 4, 5, and 6 are done very quickly, as you repeat mentally: hop, heel, hop, toe; hop, step, step, step.

Arm placement is important and you must learn to do it smoothly. While doing Step 1, the right arm, with elbow bent and hand placed about eye level, is in a vertical position near the side of the body. The left arm is in a horizontal position at chest height, in front of the body. The left hand is in a palm-down position below the right elbow. On Step 2, the right arm sweeps in front of the body and takes the horizontal position that the left arm and hand had been in, and the left arm takes the position that the right one had been holding. Right and left simply reverse positions. During Steps 3 and 4, reverse position from left to right (arms are now back in Step 1 position). On Step 5 the right hand, with

13. Irish Jig Hops, Step 3.

palm down, pushes down toward the floor just below waist height, and on Step 6 the left hand repeats this motion. In order to make your practice more interesting on the two aforementioned steps, you might enjoy doing them in dance form. To the tune of the "Irish Washerwoman" do 16 Irish Jig Steps. You will find it easier to keep in time by counting to eight twice. After this, while keeping up with your music, do four Irish Jig Hops. A complete execution counts for one time. Then turning to the right do eight more Irish Jig Steps, completing a circle on the eighth one. Then turning to the left do eight more Irish Jigs Steps, completing your circle to the left on the eighth one. To add a variety of movement you could travel forward on eight Irish Jig Steps and backward on eight.

You must practice to music and it is always more interesting to put this practicing into dance form.

A Chug is a forward movement done on either one foot or both feet by which we accent the heel drop. In the beginning we do them using both feet.

With weight evenly distributed on the balls of both feet, spring forward about three inches and force the heels of both feet to the floor. Keep your hands on your hips as you spring forward. As you push the heels down, your hands come off your hips and, with palms down near waist height, push downward to near hip height.

Later as you progress, you will learn to do Chugs on one foot only, but this must come with developed balance.

BUFFALO

An old favorite is the Buffalo, of which there are many variations. The Buffalo is usually performed traveling to one side, but I find it easier for the student at this stage to learn the step while standing in one spot, and at a later time attempt the traveling.

1. Starting with feet side by side, step on the right foot and shift your weight to that foot.

2. Brush-brush on the left foot.

3. As the left foot takes a step, shift your weight to the left foot and raise your right foot in front of the left foot near calf position, with toe pointing downward (Fig. 14).

4. You are now in a position to repeat the step on the right foot.

I find that by thinking step, brush-brush, up, the student members to bring the right foot up in the toe-down position when she places the left foot on the floor after the brush-brush. Many of you might now be able to eliminate the thought of brush-brush and replace it with the thought of shuffle, thus thinking step, shuffle, up during a Buffalo.

In Step 1 both arms are held at the side, waist height and elbows bent, with the right arm extending to the right and the left arm to the left, palms down. The left arm holds this

14. Buffalo, Step 3.

position through the entire Buffalo. At Step 2 the right hand
sweeps in toward the left shoulder about chest height, goes
up and slightly above the head, and returns to the original
side position at Step 3. You actually make a circle with the
right arm as it moves in to the left, above the head, and over
to the right side. This must be practiced until it is a smooth
motion, not overexaggerated or without continuity.

There are many ways in which one can come out of a
Buffalo and go into another step, and these we shall discuss
as they come up in our routines. You might want to practice
your Buffalos by adding a step, step. Do three Buffalos and
when you have finished Step 3 merely step down on the
right foot, and then quickly step on the left foot. You should

beth inking: step, shuffle, step; step, shuffle, step; step, shuffle, step; step (r.); step (l.).

Be sure to practice your Buffalo with both right and left feet, changing the arm motions when you change feet.

Technically a Break could be described as a two-measure motion immediately following six-measure motions. However, I feel that you will understand Breaks more clearly if they are explained as a step that breaks the continuity of the time step. There are many different types of Breaks. Since we shall soon be learning Waltz Clogs, I shall now devote time to Breaks that are associated with this particular step.

WALTZ CLOG BREAK-A

1. Standing with feet together shift weight to the left foot.
2. Kick the right foot, tapping your toe on the floor as you kick forward.
3. Hop on the left foot after this kick, turning your body slightly to the left on this hop.
4. Return the right foot to the original starting position with a step while returning the body to a straight forward position, weight on the right foot.
5. Repeat with left foot.

You should mentally repeat: kick, hop, step; kick, hop, step.

Arms are at the side of the body, elbows bent, hands nicely posed, palms down, right arm extending to the right, left extending to the left at waist height.

WALTZ CLOG BREAK-B

1. Standing with feet together hop to the heels of both feet, weight evenly distributed on both heels. This creates a forward motion.
2. Step back on right foot.
3. Step back on left foot.

Mentally you should be repeating: heels, step step; heels, step step.

Arms are held at waist height, elbows bent, in a horizontal position with palms down and fingers pointing to the front.

On Step 1 flip hands back so the fingers now point upward. On Step 2 the right hand moves back to below waist position and with palm down pushes downward. This motion is repeated with the left hand through Step 3.

One variation of the strut, called the Ball-of-Foot Strut, not only gives you another strut step, but also helps the beginner to stay on the balls of the feet. This strut entered into the picture of ballroom dancing during the days of the Boogie Woogie.

1. Stand with feet side by side, weight shifted to the left foot.

2. Rise to the balls of the feet and extend your right foot slightly forward with toe turning out to the right.

3. Pivot toe into the left, bending the right knee and immediately shifting weight onto the right foot as you toe makes a half-circle pivot and the knee straightens.

4. Weight is now on the ball of the right foot and you are ready to repeat the motion with the left foot.

The arms stay at the side of the body with hands in a palm-down position. The hand on the side of the pivoting foot pushes down slightly with the movement to below waist level.

When learning this strut you will find it easier to travel forward as you execute the step. In time it will be possible for you to stay in place if you so desire. Remember that you stay on the balls of both feet through the entire movement.

STRETCH STRUT

To add another strut variation to your accomplishments the Stretch Strut, which is a variation of the Simple Strut, should be easy for you to grasp at this point.

1. Stand with feet side by side, with weight on the left foot.

2. Stretch the right foot, with leg straight, to the front, where the toe taps the floor.

3. With weight remaining on the left foot, pull the right leg back to the side of the left foot and drop the heel.

4. Starting with the right foot do a Simple Strut forward

shifting weight to the right foot after it is completed. Repeat the step using the left foot.

You might think: stretch front, pull back, strut, as you go through your motions.

Different arm motions may be used for this. I find the most colorful and yet the easiest one is for the right arm to follow the right leg motion through the stretch, moving front and back. The left arm is at the side, waist height, with bent elbow and hand extending to the left of the body, with palm down. When doing the Simple Strut use your Simple Strut arm motion explained previously.

By now you should be doing the Hop, Brush-Brush, Steps and changing feet without any balance problem or loss of timing. In order to further perfect the Shuffle and your balance, you should now add the One-Foot Hop Shuffles. I would suggest that in the beginning you place both hands on your hips, for this will aid balance and also look nice.

ONE-FOOT HOP SHUFFLES

1. Feet are side by side and weight shifts to the left foot.
2. Hop on the left foot, raising the right foot off the floor about two inches.
3. Execute a brush-brush with the right foot.
4. Hop again on the left foot.
5. *Hop again on the left foot.* (This is hard for the beginning student to remember. There are two consecutive hops on the left foot through this combination.)
6. Execute a brush-brush again with the right foot. After practicing this with the right foot, shift weight to the right foot and repeat the steps hopping on the right foot and shuffling with the left. You should be thinking: hop, brush-brush, hop; hop, brush-brush, hop.

In order to combine the preceding steps into a form of practice lesson, I suggest you follow a pattern similar to the one outlined below.

1. Ball-of-Foot Struts, starting with the right foot: four times.

2. Sink from the ball of foot position and do four Stretch Struts, starting with the right.

3. Chug front: one time.

4. Scoot Back: one time.

5. Chug front: one time.

6. Scoot Back: one time.

7. Waltz Clog Break-B: two times.

8. Waltz Clog Break-A: two times (r.l.).

9. Buffalos: three times.

10. After the third Buffalo, instead of stepping out on the right foot from its toe-down, bent-knee position, take a hop on the left and go into One-Foot Hop Shuffles, shuffling on the right: four times.

Go through this practice exercise first starting all steps on the right foot. Then repeat the entire series starting all executions on the left foot. Since it is always wise to practice to music, you should set the above practice exercise to some type of record that you have, remembering to keep time with the beat of the music.

Turns bring a rare elegance and charm to any dance routine when they are performed properly. It takes time to develop nice-looking turns, where the body moves quickly and gracefully and the performer, like a top, spins around the stage or studio. In order to maintain a nice body line and motion, it is necessary that the performer overcomes a certain amount of the dizziness brought about by the spinning motion. We start this by training the head to turn as quickly as the body; this is called Spotting. For a description of how it works I shall use the Cross Turn, eliminating the previously learned tap, tap tap, that we used in practicing this turn in an earlier part of the text.

SPOTTING

For explanation purposes we shall turn toward the left, letting the right foot cross over in front; the decription that I shall give of Spotting techniques will be with this foot placement in mind.

You must remember, though, that it is necessary to learn

this in both directions, so after conquering it in the explained method, reverse your foot placement and put the left foot in front, turning right, with your head also reversing its position to go along with the change of foot placement.

1. As your right foot crosses in front of the left to start the turn, your head turns over the left shoulder.

2. The eyes immediately focus on an object at eye level which is in line with the body position.

3. As one goes into the orbit of the turn the eyes remain on this object until it is absolutely necessary to move them, as the turn forces the back of the body to the particular object.

4. Immediately, as the body turns, snap your head around quickly and again focus the eyes back on the object.

5. This is repeated with every turn.

Not only does Spotting help to relieve some dizziness, it adds style to the execution and also keeps the body in line while making turns. In time you will not need an object to focus on for you will be able to pick a particular spot on the wall, stage curtains, or auditorium, and readily snap your head in a quick turn and place your eyes immediately on the spot.

It is well worth the time and practice to perfect this technique, for when conquered, it elevates you from the mediocre to the accomplished when the choreographer places turns in a routine.

FOUNDATION SOFT SHOE

The motions and rhythms of the Soft Shoe are very appealing to both dancer and audience. It is necessary for one to learn the foot placement of the basic soft shoe at an early stage for it does take quite some time to develop the free-flowing motion required with this step.

1. Stand with feet together and shift weight to your left foot.

2. Slap to the right with the right foot, placing your weight on the right foot on the step.

3. Bring the left foot to a position behind the right and step on it, shifting weight to this foot and at the same time raising the right foot about one inch off the floor.

4. Now step down on the right foot, keeping it in front of the left foot, and shift weight to the right foot on this step.

5. You are now ready to start Step 2 with the left foot.

Mentally you should repeat: slap step (r.), step (l.), step (r.); slap step (l.), step (r.), step (l.).

After you have practiced this moving from right to left then you should try the same footwork traveling forward. This means that you will first slap step to the front and move forward on each step.

For the arm movements, when starting with the right foot, both arms swing in front of the body and to the right. Naturally the right arm will extend farther right than the left. The arms are held at just below chest level. They hold this position through the entire execution.

When starting Step 2 with the left foot, the arms repeat the above motion to the left, with the left arm extending farther left, of course. They hold through the entire execution. Always be sure that your hands are posed nicely through every arm placement.

Please keep in mind that this is only the basic step for Soft Shoe. In a later chapter we will go into the full Soft-Shoe Step and you will find that by knowing the Foundation Soft-Shoe Step, the soft-shoe dance can be grasped without difficulty.

SIMPLE GRAB-OFF

Another more advanced step that should be introduced to you with a simple breakdown is the Grab-Off. The pre-intermediate breakdown for this is not too difficult and assists greatly once you progress to the point of learning the more difficult Grab-Off.

1. Standing with feet together, shift weight to the left foot, raising the right foot about one inch off the floor.

2. With your right foot do a Brush-Brush, Step, crossing in front of the left foot as you do this (Fig. 15). On the step, weight goes to the right foot.

3. As you step on the right foot, the left leg stretches to the back, you bend forward from the waist (Fig. 16), and hit the left toe onto the floor as it stretches to the back.

15.   Simple Grab-Off, Step 2.   16.   Simple Grab-Off, Step 3.

4. The step of the right foot and the toe tap of the left foot must be done at exactly the same time and this is difficult to master at first. The left leg must start its stretch just prior to when the right foot touches the floor.

5. Now bring the left leg from its stretched-back position into Step 2 and repeat with the left foot.

You should be thinking: shuffle, step-toe. Stretch the leg far to the back and bend the body forward from the waist to add color and style to the execution.

While doing Step 2 the arms are crossed just above the wrists, the right arm forward when working with the right foot, and left arm forward when starting with the left foot. Of course, elbows are bent and arm placement is near waist height.

On the step-stretch of Steps 3 and 4, and as the body bends forward, the right arm extends to the right as the left arm extends to the left, with hands held at about hip height, palms turning down.

You will find that you can do a combination of Buffalos and Simple Grab-Offs which add variety to practice and help to perfect both steps. Starting with the right foot go through three Buffalos. When finished with Step 3 of the Buffalo go into a Simple Grab-Off with the right foot. After finishing Step 4 of the Simple Grab-Off, start your Buffalo with the left foot and go through a Simple Grab-Off on the left foot. This combination will help you to change foot positions quickly, shift weight properly, and it also will develop form and perfection with both right and left feet.

Traveling steps to right and left, front and back, change your stage placement and add interest and appeal to your routines. We have already discussed some forward and backward movements, which you can now do without difficulty; therefore, it is time to start learning side movements. You should start these movements with the Off-Stage Stomp.

OFF-STAGE STOMP

Even though you are traveling to the left or right, your body always faces front; you do not turn the body in the direction in which you are moving.

1. Stand with your feet together and shift your weight to the left foot.

2. Take a deep step to the left with the right foot, crossing in front of the left foot (Fig. 17). Drop your weight on the right foot and bend both knees.

3. Take a step on the left foot to the left, bringing it into line with your right foot, but about eight inches to the left of your right foot. Shift your weight onto the left foot, and straighten your knees.

4. Take a deep step to the left with the right foot, placing it *in back* of the left foot. Bend your knees and shift your weight to the right foot (Fig. 18).

5. Repeat the step on the left foot as you did in Step 3.

17. Off-Stage Stomp, Step 2.　18.　Off-Stage Stomp, Step 4.

Continue the entire execution as you move to the left of the stage or room. Mentally you should repeat: cross step, back step; cross step, back step. Remember to practice the combination starting with the left foot, too. In tap dancing, you must learn to use both feet with precision and coordination.

For the arm movements, the arms generally follow the footwork. They start at the sides of the body, elbows bent at waist height, with the right arm extending to the right and the left arm to the left, hands nicely posed.

As the right foot moves through Step 2, the right arm follows this movement in a slightly exaggerated motion. The shoulder moves slightly and the left arm goes into a position toward the back of the body.

As the left foot takes the Step 3 placement, the left arm

comes from behind the body to the side; the right arm also moves to the right side in the same manner as the left arm. When the right foot goes into position behind the left foot, the right arm also goes into a position behind the body.

Simply let your arms follow your foot positions in a slightly exaggerated or accented motion. Although this motion is accentuated, however, it is not an awkward motion, for arms must always be moved with grace and smooth continuity. Never use jerky placements or movements.

There are many variations of hops in tap dancing, from the very simple to the very intricate. Usually a hop in itself is not difficult, although the foot placements and arm movements appear complex. Above all, coordination is needed for any hop, since in most cases while you are hopping on one foot, the other foot is rising, shuffling, or kicking.

DOLL HOPS

Doll Hops are excellent for the pre-intermediate student. They are not especially hard to conquer and yet they develop the needed coordination of legs, feet, arms, and body for the more intricate combinations which require the use of hops.

1. Stand with your feet together. Shift your weight to the left foot.

2. As you hop on the left foot, bring the right foot up, with knee bent and toe down, to where the toe of the right foot is near the knee of the left leg (Fig. 19).

3. Step down on the right foot, shifting weight to the right foot.

4. Hop on the right foot, repeating Step 2 with the left foot.

5. Step down on the left foot, shifting weight to the left foot.

6. Hop on the left foot and repeat, starting with Step 2.

You should be thinking: step, hop, step, hop. You must remember to keep your shoulders back, tummy in, and to bring the bent knee up high with the toe down.

During the Doll Hop, the elbows are bent in the beginning,

19. Doll Hops, Step 2.

with arms held at the sides very close to the body, fingers pointing upward and palms turned in.

1. As your right leg comes up, bring the right hand back to shoulder height, palm turning in, fingers straight and stiff, as in the placement of a doll's arms.

2. As your right leg goes down to the floor, let your arm snap back to the starting position, keeping your hands and palms in the same position.

3. These arm placements are repeated with the left arm as you work with the left leg. Do not let the hands go below the elbows which are kept at waist height.

For practice purposes, it would be wise to combine some of the aforementioned combinations. Starting with the right foot go through two complete Off-Stage Stomps, traveling to the left. Starting the hop on the left foot do four Doll Hops. Go into one Simple Grab-Off starting with the right foot. Starting on the left foot from the extended leg position, go into another Simple Grab-Off. Do three Buffalos starting your step with the right foot, finishing with the step, step. Now repeat the Off-Stage Stomp, starting with the left foot and traveling to the right. These combinations will help you to use both feet and to move smoothly from one step into another without pause or hesitation. I must remind you again that it is the wise student who sets these practices to some type of music.

One of the most interesting and rhythmic tap dances is the military. This is usually done to music played in 4/4 time, with the performer imitating through the footwork drum beats, marching units, and the sound of bugle.

The basic breakdown for this should be very easy for you to grasp if you have spent enough time practicing your beginning Hop, Brush-Brush, Step, which we refer to now as Hop, Shuffle, Steps or Threes. The foot placement through the Military Basic is exactly the same. The only difference is a change of placement with the hop, which of course changes the sound of the rhythm.

MILITARY BASIC

This step is not used in military dances only. It is utilized in many different routines to numerous melodies. However, it is usually associated strongly with military dances so therefore it is referred to as the Military Basic.

1. Standing with feet together, shift your weight to the left foot.

2. Brush-brush (front and back) on the right. Keep weight on the left foot.

3. Hop on the left foot.

4. Step down on the right foot, shifting your weight to the right.

5. Repeat the exercise, starting with Step 2 and using the left foot.

For the present, you should keep both hands on your hips when doing the Military Basic, because this will aid in balance and help to keep the body straight. In time, however, this arm position will be replaced with the arms moving more or less as marching soldiers. During this step, you should be thinking: shuffle, hop, step; shuffle, hop, step; or you can use brush-brush, hop, step; brush-brush, hop, step.

Do not feel that your progress is unsatisfactory if you cannot substitute the word shuffle for brush-brush in your thinking. Some students can do this very quickly, while others require much longer. The important thing, as I have said before, is for the phrasing and the mental picture to be understood to the extent that immediate association between the two brings forth the desired movement.

ROCKS

Ankle flexes can be introduced at this point with a description of Rocks. Ankle flexibility must be developed along with flexibility in other parts of the body. This combination not only stresses ankle movements, but also reminds the student of the quick shift of weight necessary with every step.

1. Stand with feet together, and shift your weight to the left foot.

2. Hop on the left foot.

3. Shuffle (brush-brush) the right foot, crossing it in front of the left very close to the ankle (Fig. 20).

4. Step on your right foot with both feet in the position of Step 3. Weight must be distributed evenly on both feet.

5. As you finish Step 4, roll to the left, roll to the right, then again to the left and to the right, using an ankle motion only. It will take some time to develop this ankle roll, where the movement comes from the ankles only. With practice, however, you will become more adept and develop a flexible ankle movement. Be sure not to move your feet while rolling left and right; this must be done by the ankles only.

6. On the fourth roll, shift your weight to the right foot.

7. Bringing the left foot from its position behind the right foot, kick forward, hitting the tap on the floor. Your weight should still be on the right foot.

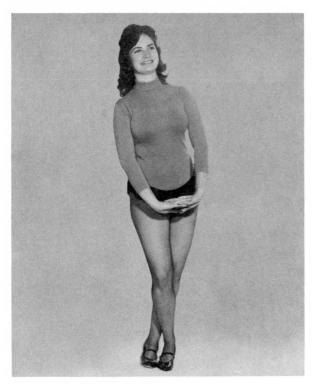

20. Rocks, Step 3.

8. Hop on the right foot, keeping your weight on this foot.

9. Step down on the left foot, shifting weight to this foot.

10. Repeat the entire series of steps again, starting with a hop on the right foot.

You should be thinking: hop, shuffle, rock, rock, rock, rock, kick, hop, step.

The arms are positioned at the side of the body in the beginning, with elbows bent and the right arm extending to the right, left arm to the left. Hold this position through Steps 2 and 3, then bring the arms into a position in front of the body at waist height, with palms down and fingers entwined. Keep this position through the rolls, then return your arms to the original position through the rest of the combination.

21. Runs, Step 2.   22. Runs, Step 4.

RUNS

Going hand and hand with Rocks in developing quick weight shifts and foot changes are Runs. These also help with timing, for you find that the rhythm varies somewhat throughout this routine.

1. Standing with feet together, shift weight to your left foot. Hop on the left foot.

2. Shuffle the right foot (Fig. 21).

3. Hop on the left foot.

4. Extending your right foot far to the back, hit the toe on the floor. Weight is still on your left foot (Fig. 22).

5. Bring the right foot from its extended position up to a

position next to the left foot, and step on the right foot, shifting weight to the right.

6. As you do Step 5, extend the left foot back and hit the toe on the floor.

7. As the left foot comes up to a position next to the right foot, step on the left foot and extend the right backward in an elevated position. *Do not hit the toe.* During this step, the body leans forward from the waist as the leg is raised in an elevated position to the rear.

8. Bring the right foot back from the elevated position, stepping on it and shifting weight to the right, as the left foot extends backward in an elevated position.

9. Repeat Step 8, with the left foot coming back into position and the right foot extending to the rear.

10. Now start again with Step 1, hopping on the left foot. You do not alternate feet as you start the combination again.

During Steps 7, 8, and 9, you are going through a running motion, slightly exaggerating the leg extension to the back. Thus a tap sound here is brought about only when you step from one foot to the other. You should be thinking: shuffle (brush-brush), hop toe, step toe, and run, run, run. The Runs must be done quickly, without pause.

Your arms should be positioned at your sides, waist height, elbows bent, with the right arm going to the right and the left to the left, palms down.

1. Hold the beginning arm position through Step 6.

2. On the run, run, run motion, the arms are positioned in front of the body near waist height, elbows bent, right hand pointing to the left and left hand pointing to the right.

3. Using the entire arm for the motion, move your arms left, right, left in order to simulate a running action.

You will find that Runs require good balance, quick movements, and smooth coordination. You will also find that body placement is very essential to the overall appearance of the step. Remember to lean forward from the waist as you kick your legs backward in the running motion. Then, as you start the hop, shuffle again, straighten your shoulders. You must remember many things when doing Runs, and the only way to do so is through repeated practice.

If you have devoted the proper amount of practice time to the past two chapters, you should find that your efforts have been rewarded by improved ability. Your exercise periods have limbered muscles and helped to develop smooth, coordinated movements. You have acquired a sense of rhythm, making it possible for you to visualize a step to the music and music changes, thus eliminating the need for concentration on counting. You should also now be able to hop and shuffle without losing your balance, and your arms should move into position gracefully and almost automatically. You have learned a great deal so far. However, do not progress to other steps and combinations until you thoroughly understand and can perform the previous ones.

The following routine should be readily understood and memorized without any problems, and will serve as a review of the steps you have studied thus far.

ROUTINE: Doll Dance to "The Wedding of the Painted Doll"
4/4 meter time, met beat 132
4-bar introduction
64 bars
2: 01 minutes

Immediately following the introduction, start from the right of the stage and enter.

1. Stretch Strut: three times. Do to three 4-counts.
2. Simple Strut: four times (r. l. r. l.). Do to one 4-count.
3. Military Basic: four times (r. l. r. l.). Do to one 4-count.
4. Repeat Step 3. Do to one 4-count.
5. Foundation Soft Shoe, traveling forward: four times (r.l.r.l.). Do to one 4-count.
6. Pull Back: four times (r. l. r. l.). Do to one 4-count.
7. Military Basic: four times (r. l. r. l.). Do to one 4-count.
8. Doll Hop: four times (r. l. r. l.). Do to one 4-count.
9. Military Basic, turning to the left and placing your back to the audience: four times. Do to one 4-count.
10. Foundation Soft Shoe, with your back to the audience and traveling toward the back of the stage: four times. Do to one 4-count.

11. Military Basic, turning to the left and ending up facing the audience: four times. Do to one 4-count.

12. Foundation Soft Shoe, traveling forward: four times. Do to one 4-count.

13. Off-Stage Stomp, traveling to the left of the stage and starting with the right foot: two times. Do to one 4-count.

14. Toe Points, turning left and placing your back to the audience and starting with the right foot: four times. Do to one 4-count.

15. Military Basic, turning left and finishing with your right side facing the audience: four times. Do to one 4-count.

16. Foundation Soft Shoe, traveling to the right of the stage with your right side to the audience: four times. Do to one 4-count.

17. Military Basic, turning left and finishing with your right side to the audience: four times. Do to one 4-count.

18. Foundation Soft Shoe, traveling to the left of the stage with your right side to the audience: four times. Do to one 4-count.

19. Military Basic, turning to the left and placing back to the audience: four times. Do to one 4-count.

20. Off-Stage Stomp, with your back to the audience: two times. Do to one 4-count.

21. Military Basic, turning to the left to face the audience: four times. Do to one 4-count.

22. Off-Stage Stomp, traveling to the left of the stage and starting with the right foot: two times. Do to one 4-count.

23. Rocks, starting each time on the left foot and shuffling on the right foot: two times. Do to two 4-counts.

24. Runs, starting each time with a hop on the left foot and a shuffle on the right foot: two times. Do to two 4-counts.

25. Military Basic, in place: four times. Do to one 4-count.

26. Doll Hop, in place: four times. Do to one 4-count.

27. Stretch Strut, turning to the left: two times. Do to two 4-counts. (*Bow.*)

You will notice that there are a total of thirty-two 4-counts in the routine, with a total of sixty-four bars on the record. Therefore, you know that you count 1–2–3–4 throughout the number. You will also notice that you do two complete Off-Stage Stomps to one 4-count. This means that you would do the cross step to the count of 1 and then do the back step to the count of 2, and repeat the same for the counts of 3 and 4.

I would like to encourage you to go through the next routine completely on your own as far as the count is concerned. Do not refer to the count I have set unless it is absolutely necessary. I will not place the count next to the steps, but rather at the end of the routine. See if you can proceed through the routine, automatically recognizing your count and feeling your step changes to the music.

This routine is a strutty dance set to a pleasant tune. I have used "Scalawag," a melody you will find quite enjoyable. Remember to include the arm placements which have been practiced with each step.

ROUTINE: "Scalawag"
4/4 meter time, met beat 124
2-bar introduction, $1\frac{1}{2}$ choruses
1: 41 minutes

After the introduction, enter from the right of the stage, starting on the right foot.

1. Simple Strut: two times (r. l.).
2. Ball-of-Foot Strut: four times (r. l. r. l.). Repeat these steps, starting with the Simple Strut two more times, then the Ball-of-Foot Strut, and repeat again, giving a total of three complete executions of these strut combinations for your entrance.
3. Pull Back, turning to face the audience: three times (r. l. r.), ending with a step on the left foot.
4. Hop, Shuffle, Step: two times (r. l.).
5. Jump Heel: two times.
6. Repeat Steps 4 and 5.
7. Cross and turn and tap, tap, tap: one time.
8. Buffalo, starting with a step on the right and finishing with a step on the right: three times.
9. Rocks, starting each time on the right: two times.
10. Heel Drops, in a circle, turning toward the right and starting on the right foot: four times.

11. Foundation Soft Shoe, in place: four times.

12. One-Foot Hop Shuffle, starting with a hop on the left foot and a shuffle with the right foot, and ending with a step on the right: three times.

13. Repeat Step 12, starting with a hop on the right foot and a shuffle with the left foot, and ending with a step on the left: three times.

14. Chug front and right.

15. Scoot Back into place.

16. Chug front and left.

17. Scoot Back into place.

18. Irish Jig Step: six times (r. l. r. l. r. l., ending with a step, step r. l.).

19. Digs, starting with the right foot: four times.

20. Simple Strut, forward, starting with the right foot: four times.

21. Military Basic, traveling backward, starting with the right foot: four times.

22. Digs, starting with the right foot: four times.

23. Foundation Soft Shoe, only with the right foot: two times.

24. Cross and turn, crossing with the left foot and turning toward the right. (Remember the spotting technique.)

25. Foundation Soft Shoe, only with the left foot: two times.

26. Cross and turn, crossing with the left foot and turning toward the right.

27. Rocks, starting each time with the right foot: two times. (*Bow.*)

You should use a total of 48 counts, the breakdown of which follows. The beginning two strut steps will give you a total of six 4-counts. The Simple Strut right and left equals one 4-count, and the Ball-of-Foot Strut equals another 4-count. Since you perform these two steps three times each, you have a total of six 4-counts.

Entrance steps (Step 1 and Step 2). Six 4-counts.

Step 3. Two 4-counts.

Step 4. One 4-count.

Step 5. One 4-count.

Step 6. One 4-count.

Step 7. Two 4-counts. (The cross and turn receives one 4-count, and the tap, tap, tap receives the other.)

Step 8. Two 4-counts.

Step 9. Four 4-counts. (The hop, shuffle, cross equals one 4-count, and the rock, rock equals one 4-count. Repeat steps for two 4-counts each.)

Step 10. Two 4-counts.

Step 11. Two 4-counts.

Step 12. Two 4-counts.

Step 13. Two 4-counts.

Steps 14 and 15. One 4-count.

Steps 16 and 17. One 4-count.

Step 18. Two 4-counts.

Step 19. Two 4-counts.

Step 20. Two 4-counts.

Step 21. Two 4-counts.

Step 22. Two 4-counts.

Step 23. One 4-count.

Step 24. One 4-count.

Step 25. One 4-count.

Step 26. One 4-count.

Step 27. Four 4-counts.

Do not feel too discouraged if, while attempting to count, you encountered some confusion and difficulty. Please understand that this also takes time and practice. Try to concentrate on recognizing the beat of the music and the breaks, for you must follow the music exactly. Perhaps the following format will be of some assistance to you, and help to remedy any problems you have had.

First read your routine over, giving no thought at all to the music. Next, perform the routine steps and practice them until you have memorized their place in the dance. Now play the music. Do not dance, but merely count 1–2–3–4 in time with the beat. Repeat this several times. As soon as the tune and the count are familiar to you, replay the music and this time mentally picture the dance steps of the routine to the music. Think the steps as you listen to the music. Picture in your mind the execution as you concentrate on the rhythm.

Repeat this mental exercise several times until you are confident of the step placement and the music beat.

After doing the above, play the music again and *physically* perform the dance steps to the music. The familiarity which you have gained with both the music and the steps should relieve the need for concentration on counting, and thereby eliminate frustration and disappointment. Your mind is now in control of your body and its movements, and this is the secret of good tap dancing.

4

The Student Progresses

AS YOU CONTINUE to progress you will realize how important your basics have been. Many steps in this chapter utilize these basics with different foot placement or different accent. You who have seriously dedicated yourselves and have thoroughly perfected the steps and combinations in the past chapters will find that as we delve into military dancing, waltz clogs, and soft-shoe dancing, the arm placements and body stances are automatic, thus allowing you to concentrate on the proper foot placement and positions. This should not be too difficult either, for previous basics, which you are completely familiar with, are combined in this chapter with various hops, steps, and shuffles, and stress is placed on different tap accents and timing, giving you new steps and positions.

Again we will start with the all-important exercising, which must be maintained for proper coordination and agility. By now muscles are limber and toned and more strenuous stretches may be undertaken.

Floor exercises are designed to assist in leg stretches. They also help other parts of the body considerably because lying on the floor while exercising eliminates the concern of maintaining your balance. Of course, proper positioning throughout the exercise is most important whether you are on the floor or standing.

You lose a great deal by not doing your exercises as described, since the foot placement, the toe position, the arm placement and even the head position have all been designed to cause the right pull in the right places.

FLOOR EXERCISE: Leg Stretch (1)

1. Lie flat on your back with knees straight, arching the foot and pointing the toes in the direction of the floor.

2. Your left arm stays in position near the left side of your body.

3. Right arm extends out to the right at shoulder height.

4. Keeping both legs locked and toes pointed, push the right leg to the right and slide it upward toward the right arm. (Do not twist your body as you do this. Your left leg stays straight, toe down.) Do this slowly.

5. After you have pushed the leg as far as possible without bending either knee or losing either toe position, slowly bring the right leg back to starting position.

6. Repeat four times.

7. Change positions and put your left arm out to your side and repeat with the left leg.

It is most important that you do not bend either knee, that you do not twist the body to the right or left, and that you maintain your toe position. Do not expect to slide the leg as high as the extended arm in the beginning and hold the proper body position. This will take time and practice and you are well aware of the fact that it is not wise to overdo any exercise when first learning it.

FLOOR EXERCISE: Leg Stretch (2)

1. You are in a sitting position.

2. Bend knees and place them near chin.

3. Take hold of your right toes with your right hand, left toes with your left hand.

4. Holding the toes, slide the legs forward until they are flat on the floor.

5. Bend your head toward the knees.

6. Still grasping the toes slide the legs back to starting position.

7. Repeat four times.

In all probability you will not be able to push your legs

flat on the floor the first few times you do this exercise. Push only as far as you can without letting go of the toes. Soon the muscles will pull and limber, and you will be able to push your legs to a flat position on the floor as your head touches the knees.

Again I want to remind you not to neglect your other exercises. You must conscientiously develop good self-discipline if you are a self-taught student. If you are studying in a school, your teacher will maintain very firm class discipline. Such discipline brings forth instant reactions, which are essential in the make-up of a good tap dancer.

The Military Basic in the past chapter is your first step into the military tap dance. This dance is always the students' favorite, for the rhythm and happy melodies which accompany military dances have so much bounce they bring forth that "toetapping" feeling. Military dances also have much appeal to the audience. We Americans all love a parade, with the sound of the band, the precision of the marchers, and the cadence of the drums. This combination penetrates right into the hearts of the viewers. This is also true with military tap dances. The costume worn usually is a military cut and design, and the sound of the footwork brings to mind a colorful parade and a patriotic feeling which bubbles in the hearts of one and all.

The Military Combination that predominates in most of these dances is a combination of the Military Basic and other steps. There are five points to this combination and the student will find it easier to stay with the count and music if she learns this combination while thinking of the five points. Before the beginning breakdown, let me explain this further; this will enable you to thoroughly comprehend the breakdown. The rhythm of the Military Combination is (1) shuffle, hop, step, step, step; (2) shuffle, hop, step, step, step; (3) shuffle, hop, step; (4) shuffle, hop, step; (5) shuffle, hop, step, step, step. These five points make up the combination.

MILITARY UNIT

1. Stand with your feet together, and shift weight to the left foot.

2. Perform a Military Basic on the right foot, shifting weight to the right foot on the step.

3. Step left, shifting weight to the left foot on the step.

4. Step right, shifting weight to the right foot on the step.

5. Repeat Steps 2, 3, and 4, starting on the left foot and alternating feet.

6. Do one Military Basic on the right foot, shifting weight to the right foot on the step.

7. Do one Military Basic on the left foot, shifting weight to the left foot on the step.

8. Repeat Steps 2, 3, and 4, starting on the right foot.

This entire execution completes one Military Combination. Therefore, if a dance routine requires four Military Combinations, this means that you would go through the five points above four times.

During the execution, keep your hands moving like a marching soldier.

There are many variations of the Military Basic, which are created by merely changing the foot placement. For your convenience, these are described as Military Basic Variation-A and -B.

MILITARY BASIC VARIATION-A

1. Your weight is on the left foot.

2. Your right foot does a shuffle.

3. Hop on the left foot, with your weight still on this foot.

4. Tap your right toe on the floor, keeping your weight on the left foot.

5. Repeat again, with the right foot doing the shuffle. Do not alternate feet.

You should be thinking: shuffle, hop, toe; shuffle, hop, toe. In a routine, you might do this four times without alternating feet and possibly go from this into a Military Combination, then repeat the Military Basic Variation-A with the left foot.

As you do the footwork, your elbows should be bent, at waist height, with right arm extending to the right and left arm to the left, palms down and hands nicely posed.

In order to do this step, repeat Variation-A but replace the toe tap with a heel drop on the shuffling foot. The arm placement remains the same, and your thinking now becomes: shuffle, hop, heel; shuffle, hop, heel. Remember not to alter feet after each step.

You can also present these two basic military steps by crossing the leg in front of the foot you have hopped on, before doing the toe tap or heel drop. This change in foot placement creates an altogether different appearance in the execution of the steps.

To change your rhythm with these two variations, you might do Variation-A three times and add two toe taps with the right foot. This changes your thinking to: shuffle, hop, toe; shuffle, hop, toe; tap, tap. There is a wealth of variety in military variations, and as you practice you will probably be able to originate other foot placements.

HEEL ROLLS

Heel work plays an important role in military dancing, and you will soon learn that ankle flexibility is a necessity. Heel Rolls oftentimes emulate a group of marchers or the beat of a drum, so it is essential that they be distinct and performed in perfect time to the music.

Heel Rolls, which are called Cramp Rolls in some parts of the country, are actually used in all types of tap dancing, but they are most often associated with military dancing. They may be done in place, moving forward or backward, or traveling in a specific stage pattern.
The execution is similar to the Chug.

1. Stand with your weight distributed evenly on both feet.

2. Do a very small jump, raising the feet only an inch off the floor.

3. Land on the balls of the feet and quickly push your right heel to the floor, followed immediately by your left heel.

You should be thinking: jump, heel right, left; jump, heel right, left. The arm placement varies through this, but the beginner can try saluting with the right hand while the left hand remains on the hip.

After getting the feel of the Heel Rolls, you can change your rhythm in various ways. After doing three Heel Rolls add a step right, left. This changes your thought to: heels, heels, heels, step, step.

HEEL ROLL COMBINATION

A continuation of the preceding variation is known as the Heel Roll Combination, and is done by adding steps on the right and left.

1. Do three Heel Rolls.
2. Step on the right foot, shifting your weight to the right; step on your left foot, shifting your weight to the left.
3. Repeat Steps 1 and 2 above.
4. Do one Heel Roll.
5. Step on the right foot, step on the left foot.
6. Repeat Steps 4 and 5 above.
7. Repeat Steps 1 and 2 above.

This series of steps creates a mental picture of: heels, heels, heels, right, left; heels, heels, heels, right, left; heels, right, left; heels, right, left; heels, heels, heels, right, left.

Many turns can be used in military dancing, and you will find as you progress that you can apply turns which are described in other routines to a military number by changing the accent of the sound. One shuffle turn which is most appropriate for a student at this phase of study is a Shuffle Step Turn, which we do first on one foot, completing the circle, before reversing weight position so that we can do the same footwork using the other foot. You will find this particular step appearing in soft-shoe dances, Rhythm Bucks, and Sevens, with the tap accent on a different part of the footwork. It is a very versatile step and is called the Shuffle Step Turn, One Foot. In time you will learn to alternate feet with this turn.

SHUFFLE STEP TURN, ONE FOOT

1. Your weight is on the left foot. For demonstration purposes we will turn left, stepping on the left foot and

shuffling on the right foot. Of course, you must learn to do this with each foot, so you should also practice with the alternate foot, reversing the step and the shuffle and therefore the direction of the turn.

2. Shuffle step on the right foot, shifting your weight to the right foot on the step.

3. Step on the left foot, accenting this step.

Continue to repeat the above footwork while turning your body to the left on each step. In the beginning allow yourself eight executions to complete the turn. After you can do this, placing the proper accent on the step mentioned in Step 3 and without having to concentrate on the movements, complete the circle in six executions. Soon you will be able to make a complete circle using only four executions, which is what most routines call for.

During this execution, the right arm is in a diagonal position extending to the right and above the head. The left arm is in a diagonal position to the left, with the hand below the hip. The body leans back and to the left as you do the turn to the left. Of course, these arm placements are reversed when you are turning to the right.

Your thought through this step is: shuffle, step, *step;* remember to place an accent on the last step.

Many years ago the term "slap" was used to define an emphatic back-brush movement, while the word "flap" was used to describe the corresponding forward movement. Since the footwork is exactly the same, however, teachers began using just one term to describe the movement, adding to the name of the term the direction, either forward or backward.

In modern teaching, the term "slap" is used for both, and these you should be familiar with already, for they are part of an exercise mentioned in the very first chapter. Slaps changing from forward to backward are often used in military routines, as well as in other types of choreography.

FORWARD SLAPS

1. Rise to the balls of your feet, and shift your weight to the left foot.

2. Do a quick brush (slap) step forward with the right foot, and shift your weight to this foot.

3. Repeat this with the left foot, as the movement carries you forward.

4. Be sure to remain on the balls of your feet.

Your elbows should be bent, with the right arm extending to the right, left arm to the left at waist height; the shoulder on the side of the slapping foot moves slightly forward with the execution. Hands are posed with palms down.

You should be thinking: slap step; slap step.

BACKWARD SLAPS

1. Use the same weight shifts described for the Forward Slap, but direct the motion of the slap backward instead of to the front.

2. Your mental picture and arm placement should remain the same. You are merely changing the direction of your movement.

I would suggest that you do four Forward Slaps, immediately followed by four Backward Slaps. Repeat this exercise a number of times until the motion is fixed in your mind and there is no hesitation or pause as you change directions.

Next you should practice the slaps by breaking the motion with a Military Basic. Do four Forward Slaps, four Backward Slaps, four Military Basics, and repeat. If you do not have any military music at this time, you might think about or hum the tune of "Alexander's Ragtime Band." This will give you an idea of the rhythm and count.

One-Foot Hop Shuffles, mentioned earlier in Chapter Three, are often used in military dances, with the accent being placed on the hop mentioned in Step 4 of the breakdown for this execution. This rhythm is usually broken by a brush-brush, hop, step. Starting with a hop on the left foot and a shuffle on the right foot, do three One-Foot Hop Shuffles, keeping your weight on the left foot. Shuffle on the right foot, hop on the left foot, and then step down on the right foot, shifting your weight to that foot. Now repeat the series starting the hop on the left foot and shuffling on the right foot again.

One of the most exciting steps which is used in military dancing is the Rat-a-Tat, which sounds like a machine gun and, once learned, is done at a very rapid speed. It is difficult to explain, however, and each step must be followed slowly and closely in the beginning, for it would be very easy to lose the entire step if, in haste, you should overlook one part of the explanation.

1. With your weight on the left foot, raise your right foot about one inch off the floor.

2. Chug forward on the left foot.

3. At the same time, shuffle your right foot.

4. Hop on your left foot, keeping your weight on this foot.

5. Repeat Steps 3 and 4 a total of three times.

6. Do a shuffle on the right foot.

7. Repeat again, starting with Step 2 and going through to Step 6.

8. Repeat Steps 2, 3, and 4.

9. Shuffle on the right foot.

10. Repeat Steps 2, 3, 4, and 6.

11. Repeat again, starting with Step 2 and going through Step 6.

This entire combination is one complete execution. Therefore, if a routine calls for four Rat-a-Tats, you would do this entire combination four times. Remember that your weight remains on the left foot during the entire execution.

You should be thinking: *chug,* shuffle, hop, shuffle, hop, shuffle, hop, shuffle; *chug,* shuffle, hop, shuffle, hop, shuffle, hop, shuffle; *chug,* shuffle, hop, shuffle, hop, shuffle, hop, shuffle; *chug,* shuffle, hop, shuffle; *chug,* shuffle, hop, shuffle; *chug, shuffle, hop, shuffle, hop, shuffle, hop, shuffle.* You are accenting the Chug and doing the Shuffle with rapid continuity, keeping your foot very close to the floor and producing a rat-a-tat sound.

When considering the arm placement for the Rat-a-Tat, we must think of assisting balance as well as creating an attractive appearance. Elbows are bent and the right arm extends to the right, the left arm to the left, at waist position.

As you Chug, the left shoulder pushes forward and the left arm follows this movement and then returns to its original position on the shuffle.

In the beginning you will find that you move forward on this step, since the Chug is a forward movement. Actually, though, you should stay in place and not travel at all through the Rat-a-Tat; in time you will learn to move the left foot back to its original position on the first hop. This should not concern you in the beginning phase. Concentrate on executing quick shuffles and hops and you will eventually find that you no longer move forward, for you are automatically bringing the left foot back into place on the first hop.

The Rat-a-Tat is also very tiring when you are first learning it. You will find that the fast shuffles done on the right foot quickly tire that foot and leg until you can build up endurance. Should you try to continue practicing when your legs are tired, you will not be able to produce the desired sound effect or maintain your balance well. It is therefore best to do something more restful at this time, and then return to the Rat-a-Tat when your legs are no longer tired.

We have touched on many combinations and steps applicable to military routines. You should know these thoroughly, both physically and mentally, before attempting the following routines. In these routines, I have utilized only previously explained steps. If you have practiced these well, the following routines will then be easy for you to understand and perform.

ROUTINE: "Alexander's Ragtime Band"
　　　　　4/4 meter time, met beat 160
　　　　　3 chord, 4-bar introduction
　　　　　1: 40 minutes

There are 64 bars in the song, so you will have a total of sixty-four 4-counts.

1. Starting on the right foot, with weight on the left foot, shuffle (r.), hop (l.), step (r.), step (l.), step (r.). Alternate feet and do a total of four times. Do to four 4-counts.

2. Military Basic: four times. Do to two 4-counts.

3. Heel Rolls: four times. Do to two 4-counts.

4. One-Foot Hop Shuffles, starting on the right foot and finishing the series with a Grab-Off: three times. Do to two 4-counts.

5. Repeat Step 4, starting on the right foot and finishing the series with a Grab-Off. Do to two 4-counts.

6 Military Basic Variation-B, starting on the right foot: one time. Do to one 4-count.

7. Military Basic Variation-B, starting on the left foot: one time. Do to one 4-count.

8. Heel Rolls: four times. Do to two 4-counts.

9. Military Unit: two times. Do to eight 4-counts.

10. Military Basic Variation-A, crossing in front, shuffling with the right foot, and ending with a step: four times. Do to four 4-counts.

11. Repeat Step 10, crossing in front of the right foot and shuffling with the left foot: four times. Do to four 4-counts.

12. Military Units, turning to the right and starting on the right foot: two times. Do to eight 4-counts.

13. Simple Strut, traveling forward: two times. Do to one 4-count.

14. March stiffly forward (1. r. 1. r.). Do to one 4-count.

15. Grab-Off, starting on the right: two times. Do to two 4-counts.

16. Repeat the step in Step 1 of the routine, moving to the back of the stage: four times (r. l. r. l.). Do to four 4-counts.

17. Foundation Soft Shoe, traveling forward: four times. Do to two 4-counts.

18. Toe Points, to the back: four times (r. l. r. l.). Do to two 4-counts.

19. Repeat Step 1 of the routine: two times (r. l.). Do to two 4-counts.

20. Cross Turn to the left, crossing the right foot in front: two turns. Do to two 4-counts.

21. Repeat the Cross Turn, this time turning to the right and crossing the left foot in front: two turns. Do to two 4-counts.

22. Military Basic: four times. Do to two 4-counts.

23. Heel Drops: four times. Do to two 4-counts. (*Bow*).

ROUTINE: "American Patrol"
    4/4 meter time, met beat 174
    4-bar introduction
    64 bars
    1:25 minutes

1. Military Unit: two times.
2. Hop (l.), brush-brush (r.), hop (l.): three times. Brush-brush (r.), hop (l.), step (r.): one time.

Repeat this combination hopping on the right foot and shuffling on the left foot. Repeat again hopping on the left and repeat again hopping on the right. You should be thinking: hop, shuffle, hop; hop, shuffle, hop; hop, shuffle, hop; shuffle, hop, step, through each combination.

3. Heels, step, step: two times.
4. Brush-brush, hop, step, starting with the right foot and alternating from the left to the right to the left: four times. Toe Points to the front, starting on the right foot and alternating to the left foot: four times (r. l. r. l.).
5. Brush-Brush, Step on the right foot, then step on the left foot while turning to the left, making a complete circle with seven executions. Then Lunge forward on the right foot, shifting weight to the right on the eighth count.
6. Reverse Step 5, doing the Brush-Brush, Step on the left foot, then stepping on the right foot while turning to the right, making a complete circle with seven executions. Then Lunge forward on the left foot, shifting weight to the left on the eighth count.
7. Heels, step, step (drop both heels to the floor and step right, step left): two times.
8. Starting with the right foot, do a brush-brush, hop, step four times, alternating feet, and repeat the heels, step, step two times.
9. Brush-brush, hop, step, starting on the right foot and alternating to the left foot: four times.
10. Heels, heels, heels, step, step, moving forward: two times.
11. Toe Points to the back, starting with the right foot and turning to the right, making a circle with four points.

12. Runs: one time.
13. Military Unit: two times.
14. Runs: two times.
15. Grab-Off: two times.
16. Heels, heels, heels, step, step. (*Bow*).

You will find now that routines are much easier to read and follow, and you should form a mental picture of the steps as you review them. The time and patience you have spent on practicing should be really beginning to show, and you should be able to move quickly though a routine if you have perfected the steps learned previously.

As students progress through the intermediate stages of tap dancing, the Waltz Clog quickly becomes a favorite step. It has a definite, floaty rhythm, and is done in 3/4 time. Often the Waltz Clog is referred to as Fives, since the tap count is 1–2–3–4–5. The older name originated when performers used to wear clogs consisting of wooden soles and heels made of maple. Today metal taps are used.

It is difficult in the beginning for the student to develop the floaty tap beat of the Waltz Clog. The normal tendency is to accent the tap on the 1, 3, and 5 counts, thus losing the desired unstressed sound. However, with practice and concentration the floaty rhythm can be achieved, and Waltz Clogs or Fives will become a favorite step.

Body positioning is understandably important with this step, since a naturally graceful movement must be developed. Remember as you go through the execution to stay on your tiptoes and not on the flat of your feet. This is something which the intermediate student should definitely have mastered by now.

WALTZ CLOG

1. Step slightly to the left on your left foot, keeping your weight on this foot.

2. Brush-brush, step on your right foot, ending with your weight on the right foot.

3. Step on your left foot, shifting your weight to this foot.

4. Step slightly to the right on your right foot, shifting your weight to this foot (Fig. 23).

Step right, raise left.   *Brush.*   *Brush.*   *Step left, weight on left. Raise right as left steps.*   *Step right, weight on right.*

23.   Waltz Clog, Step 4.

5. Brush-brush, step on your left foot, ending with your weight on the left foot.

6. Step on the right foot, keeping your weight on this foot.

You should shift your weight quickly from one foot to the other without pausing, and you should be thinking: 1–2–3–4–5, smoothly, without accent on any one count in either your thought or execution.

ONE-FOOT FIVES OR WALTZ CLOGS

1. Step on your left foot, shifting your weight to this foot.

2. Brush-brush, step on your right foot; do not shift your weight completely to this foot.

3. Step on your left foot.

4. Again step on your left foot, and then repeat the above steps.

When practicing One-Foot Fives, vary your execution slightly by making a circle to the right while doing the steps with your right foot, and a circle to the left while doing them with your left foot. This helps keep the rhythm, and adds a little more style to the presentation of this particular step.

By now, a natural feeling for arm placement should be developing. You will find that elbows at waist height with arms extending to the left and right respectively, with palms down and fingers nicely posed, will be the most natural and comfortable position for you when doing the Waltz Clog. When kicks, or breaks as they are sometimes called, appear in a routine, your arms follow gracefully along with the leg movements.

Along with being a very rhythmic step, the Waltz Clog can add a great deal of audience appeal to a routine through novel arrangements. This step can be done in a number of different presentations, thereby creating a great deal of versatility for the dancer.

One of the most interesting and challenging novelty dances is the Jump Rope Dance. The performer actually jumps rope while executing the various steps of the dance. This requires a great deal of coordination and concentration on the part of the dancer, but even a student who has only reached the intermediate stage can perform this dance after some practice.

The floaty rhythm of the Waltz Clog or Fives is about the only tap-dancing step which can be easily performed with a jump rope. The Waltz Clog Breaks and Heel Combinations explained earlier fit in well with the movement of the rope. After sufficient practice, you will learn to coordinate your foot movements and the rope movement with ease and grace.

Start practicing first with just the Waltz Clog step and the rope and then, as you progress with this, add the Waltz Clog Breaks and Heel Combinations.

The routines which are explained at the end of this chapter are designed with novelty dancing in mind. Do not be discouraged, however, if you miss a tap or a rope jump in the beginning, because only with extensive practice can you perfect a skill, and this is particularly true with the Jump Rope Dance. Remember that the rope should pass under your feet as you do the step; as the rope goes up and behind your body, do the brush-brush. When the rope drops in front of your feet for the step, step, quickly step over the rope. Do

24. Stair Dance, Step 1.

it slowly in the beginning, and you will soon perfect the various movements.

Stair dancing, another type of novelty presentation, also utilizes the Waltz Clog. Again, the floaty rhythm of the step makes the movements easy and fun. I would suggest practicing the Waltz Clog or Fives step until confidence develops. At that time, go into the Breaks and Heel Combinations.

In the Stair Dance, one foot is usually on a stair step above the other. For explanation purposes, I have outlined a breakdown of the dance starting with the right foot and using four stairs. Start with your feet together on the first stair.

1. Step on your right foot to the second stair (Fig. 24).
2. Brush-brush your left foot on the first stair.
3. Step on your left foot to the third stair.

4. Step on your right foot to the third stair, so that both feet are momentarily on the same stair.

5. Step on your left foot to the fourth stair.

6. Brush-brush your right foot on the third stair.

7. Step on your right foot to the fourth stair, so that again both feet are on the same stair.

After some practice, you will find that you can climb a stair on each step of the dance. This does take time, but is worth mastering. By using imaginative and clever choreography, one can create a very nice Stair Dance using Fives, Breaks, and Heel Combinations. Since you are already familiar with the arm placements used with these steps, the only thing you must really concentrate on is your count.

You will notice through the following Waltz Clog routine that I have included steps which you have also done in the military tap dances. With just a slight variation of your beat, these same steps can be used just as effectively through the floaty movement of the Waltz Clog dance as they can be through the precise beat of the military tap dance.

ROUTINE: "Take Me Out to the Ball Game"
         3/4 meter time, met beat 168
         4-bar introduction
         96 bars
         1: 43 minutes

1. Waltz Clogs, starting with a step to the left on the left foot: six times.

2. Waltz Clog Break-A, starting with the right foot, then the left foot: two times.

3. Cross Turn and tap, tap, tap, tap: one time.

4. Waltz Clogs, starting with a step to the right on the right foot: four times.

5. Waltz Clog Break-B: four times.

6. One-Foot Fives, stepping on the left foot and brushing with the right foot, while turning to the left to make a complete circle: four times, making a full circle.

7. Rock, crossing the right foot in front of the left foot: one time.

8. Waltz Clogs, starting on the right foot: two times.

9. Waltz Clog Break-A, starting on the right foot: two times.

10. Runs, starting on the right foot: two times.

11. Waltz Clogs: eight times.

12. Waltz Clog Break-A, starting the kick with your right foot and turning to the right: eight times, alternating from the right foot to the left foot and making a circle, ending on the eighth kick by facing your audience again.

13. Brush-brush hop, brushing on the right foot only and hopping on the left foot only, stepping on the right foot to finish the combination: one time.

14. Slap, step, step on the left foot only: four times, finishing the combination with a step on the left. Your weight is on the right foot, then slap, step on the left foot shifting your weight to the left, then step on the right foot, shifting your weight back to the right foot.

15. Waltz Clogs, starting with a step to the right on your right foot: four times.

16. Brush-brush on your right foot, then hop on your left foot: two times, finishing with a step on your right foot and shifting your weight to that foot.

17. Waltz Clogs, moving to the right of the stage and starting on the right foot: six times.

18. Waltz Clog Break-A, starting with the left foot: two times.

19. Waltz Clogs, moving to the left of the stage and starting on the left foot: six times.

20. Waltz Clog Break-A, starting with the right foot: two times.

21. Waltz Clog Break-B, making a complete circle turning to the right: four times.

22. Cross Turn and tap, tap, tap, tap: one time.

23. Brush-brush on your right foot, then hop on your left foot: two times, finishing with a step on your right foot.

24. Repeat Step 23, brushing on the left and hopping on the right: two times.

25. Waltz Clogs, moving to the right of the stage on the right foot: two times.

26. Grab-Off: one time. (*Bow*).

This routine requires some quick footwork, but by now you should have reached the point where your mind can quickly grasp the routine and control your body through each movement.

At this stage, you should have mastered the basic steps and timing and, therefore, can readily apply yourself to quick weight changes from right to left with very little concentration. Also, your arm movements should gracefully follow your body movements without requiring much thinking, and it should be easier for you to time your taps to the beat of the music. Yes, if you have studied at all diligently, you have now progressed through the intermediate stage of tap dancing, have added some novelty dancing to your repertoire, and are ready to accept the challenge of pre-advanced combinations.

5

Pre-advanced Combinations

THERE IS much to be said for soft-shoe dancing. In my opinion it is sheer beauty, as graceful as the fawn and as rhythmic as the bongo beat. The dance was originally performed with sand on the floor. In most cases, this has now been replaced by the metal tap; however, the tap sound is never heavily accented. The dance is set to a slow 4/4 time, where the accent is on essence, a basic movement which contains many varied patterns and combinations.

To reach perfection in soft-shoe dancing one must sway gently and gracefully without an over-exaggerated motion or sound. The rhythm of each combination, each step, is the same. The body must float as lightly as a feather, and the arms and torso movements must move as gently as a branch in a spring breeze.

Although soft-shoe dancing is very relaxing it does take a great deal of practice and time before the dancer can perform it with confidence. However, it is well worth perfecting, for there is nothing more satisfying or rewarding than knowing you can perform a soft-shoe dance with the desired grace of body movement along with the intricate footwork.

Many professional dancers include a soft-shoe dance as their encore. The audience enjoys it very much and although the footwork is difficult, the slower speed of the music is very restful after performing a fast Buck or military dance.

Just as a singer's mark of distinction is on phrasing, the soft-shoe dancer concentrates on timing.

25. Soft Shoe, Step 1.   26. Soft Shoe, Step 2.

As you will remember, we did discuss the Foundation Soft Shoe in Chapter Three, and after practicing this you will be a little more familiar with the material we shall now introduce.

SOFT SHOE

1. Your weight is on the left foot (Fig. 25).
2. Slap, step to the right on your right foot, quickly shifting your weight to the right on this foot (Fig. 26).
3. Slap, step on your left foot behind the right, quickly shifting your weight to the left on this step.
4. Step quickly on the right foot.
You should be thinking: slap, step; slap, step; step. After

going through the above execution, repeat the action to the left, starting on your left foot. Remember that the second foot always places itself behind the foot that started the soft-shoe step; the body and the footwork move right when slapping toward the right, and to the left when slapping toward the left. Your body sways with the foot movements. Both arms sway to the right when moving to the right, at about chest height, with palms down and hands attractively posed. When slapping toward the left, your arms sway toward the left.

There are many turns which adapt well to soft-shoe dancing. As you develop a feeling for the music, by changing footwork, many of your previously learned turns can be utilized.

PADDLE TURNS

One of the most interesting and showy turns is the Paddle Turn. The body placement for this turn appears difficult, so remember that along with the footwork, it is most important for you to concentrate on arm placement as well.

1. Stand with your weight on the right foot.

2. Slap, step to the back on the left foot, quickly shifting your weight from the right foot to the left foot.

3. Step on your right foot, quickly shifting your weight to this foot.

You are turning your body to the left as you do the above steps, and your count is 1–2–3, rapidly, with a slight accent on the three. Lean your shoulder back as you stretch your left arm high, with your elbow at eye level. Your knees should be slightly bent so that your right arm extends down with the hand near knee level.

In keeping with the rhythm of the Soft Shoe, you can vary your sound using the Shuffle Step Turn explained in Chapter Four; do the same execution in time with the soft-shoe rhythm.

SOFT-SHOE KICK HOPS

Lithe kicks and hops add appeal to soft-shoe dancing, and you will find that the Soft-Shoe Kick Hop has a sharp tap sound but at the same time is very restful.

1. Kick your right foot forward, slapping your toe.

2. With your weight on the left foot, hop on this foot, keeping your weight on the left through the hop.

3. Crossing your right foot in front of the left, slap back on the right foot, and then step down, shifting your weight to the right foot.

4. Repeat these steps, starting with the left foot.

You should be thinking: kick, hop; slap, step; kick, hop; slap, step.

Starting with your hands at waist height with elbows bent, bring your hands inward and up over the head, making a complete circle. Your right hand moves in and out to the right, in a complete circle; your left hand moves in and out to the left, also in a complete circle. Remember that this must be done gracefully and the arm movements must be completely finished at the end of the step.

CHORUS KICKS

1. With your weight on the left foot, tap your right toe on the floor while hopping on your left foot.

2. Kick your right leg high and to the front, as you hop again on your left foot.

3. While stepping down on your right foot, shift your weight to the right and at the same time tap your left toe on the floor.

4. Hop on your right foot and kick your left leg high and to the front.

Remember to pose your foot attractively while doing the kicks. Your elbows should be at waist height, with your right arm extending to the right, left arm to the left, hands posed and palms down. You might add some body movement by shifting your right shoulder forward when doing the kick with your right leg, and the left shoulder forward when kicking with the left leg.

SWANEES

Swanees and variations of Swanees can be found in almost any soft-shoe routine, so it is wise to learn this step and remember it well.

1. With weight on the left, hop on the left foot.

2. Shuffle, step on the right foot behind the left foot, shifting the weight to the right on the step.

3. Step left, quickly shifting weight to the left, with the left foot in front of the right foot.

4. Step on the right foot, quickly shifting weight, with the right foot behind the left foot.

5. On the left foot slap back and step, placing the left foot now behind the right, with weight on the left foot.

6. Step right, shifting weight quickly to the right, with the right foot in front.

7. Step left, shifting weight quickly to the left, with the left foot behind the right foot.

8. Repeat Steps 5, 6, and 7 using the right foot.

9. Step left, with weight on the left foot.

You should be thinking: hop shuffle, step, step, step, slap back, step, step, slap back, step, step, step.

Your previous exercising should have helped considerably in molding you into shape for soft-shoe dancing. There is considerable amount of toe-heel work in this type of dancing, and one needs quick ankle flexes and limber legs.

RIVER-BOAT SHUFFLE

A combination of shuffles and heelwork is the River-Boat Shuffle. Once perfected, the tap sound with this step is very interesting. Remember to keep your feet very close to the floor.

1. Your weight should be on the left foot.

2. Shuffle your right foot, crossing it in front of the left foot.

3. Lift your left heel and then hit the floor, keeping your weight on the left foot.

4. Slap toe, heel with your right foot.

5. Shift your weight to the right on the heel slap.

6. Bring your left foot out from behind the right foot, and repeat the execution starting with the left foot.

7. While doing the above steps, you should be traveling forward.

Your arms should be held at waist height with elbows bent and palms down, and should follow the foot movements.

A step that takes some concentration in the beginning is the Diller. The quick shifts of weight with the heelwork cause some difficulty if you try to do this step too fast while learning. Take each breakdown slowly until you have a mental grasp of the step.

1. Your weight is on the left foot.

2. Tap your right toe slightly to the front.

3. Raise and then lower your left heel.

4. Quickly shift your weight to the right, with your right heel hitting the floor on the weight shift.

5. Repeat this action, starting the tap on the left foot at Step 2.

6. Repeat again, starting the tap on the right foot.

7. Kick your left leg and step on your left foot, shifting your weight on the left.

8. Step on your right foot, shifting your weight to the right.

Repeat the entire combination starting with the left toe at Step 2. You should be thinking: toe, heel, heel; toe, heel, heel; toe, heel, heel; kick, step, step. Your count is 1 and 2, 3 and 4, 5 and 6, 7 and 8.

SOFT-SHOE TURNS

This is a very restful and easy turn in soft-shoe dancing. It merely uses a step which you have been doing in place; by turning the body, you create a step which appears altogether different. Be sure to follow the rhythm while practicing this step.

Do not start turning while you are first learning the step. Practice it in place until you feel sure of your movements and timing.

1. With weight on your left foot, kick your right foot, tapping the toe on the floor very lightly as you do the kick.

2. Hop on your left foot, with weight on the left.

3. Step on your right foot, shifting your weight to the right.

Repeat the above movements, starting with the left foot. Do not move your feet high off the floor. Practice in place until you are able to keep up with a quick 1–2–3 count without losing your timing, then start the body turning either left or right as you do the execution.

COMBINATION TRIPLES FRONT AND BACK

1. With your weight on the left foot, brush-brush, step with your right foot, crossing in front of the left foot. Shift weight quickly to the right.

2. Step on your left foot, shifting your weight to this foot.

3. Repeat Step 1, putting your right foot in back of the left foot.

4. Step on your left foot.

After going through the above steps, remember to reverse feet and practice the shuffle on the left and the step on the right.

DRAW SPRING WITH HEELWORK

Borrowing a step from the ballet world, we often use Draw Springs or *ballet sata* in soft-shoe dancing. This is a step which requires considerable coordination and must be executed in a graceful, floaty manner. Understandably, it originated in the ballet field, but has been adapted to tap dancing by the addition of slaps and heel movements.

1. With weight on your left foot, slap forward with your right foot, shifting your weight to the right foot.

2. Slap forward on your left foot, shifting weight to the left foot.

3. Slap forward on your right foot, keeping your weight on the right foot, then hop on this foot while extending your left leg straight back (Fig 27).

4. Step on your left foot, shifting weight to this foot.

5. Do a toe, heel step with your right foot.

6. Step on your left foot, traveling backward.

7. Repeat Steps 5 and 6 three times.

To make your practice a bit more interesting, I will take these Soft-Shoe steps and combinations from other chapters, and set them to a soft-shoe dancing routine. It is always more fun to practice when you feel as if you are performing a dance.

27.
Draw Spring with
Heelwork, Step 3.

ROUTINE: "For Me and My Gal"
met beat 102
3 chord, 4-bar introduction
2 choruses

On the introduction, do Simple Struts on the stage.

1. Soft-Shoe steps: eight times.

2. Paddle Turns, turning to the left using the left foot for the slap: eight times, for a total of two complete turns.

3. Slap down, step left, step right: two times, alternating feet.

4. Toe Point on the left foot behind the right foot and to the right, then step on your left foot, placing it beside your right foot and shifting your weight to the left foot.

5. Toe Point on the right foot behind the left foot and to the left, then step on your right foot, placing it beside your left foot and shifting your weight to the right foot.

6. Repeat Steps 4 and 5.

7. Soft-Shoe steps: four times.

8. Cross Turn and tap, tap, tap, tap: one time.

9. River-Boat Shuffles, moving to the right of the stage: eight times.

10. Soft-Shoe steps: four times.

11. Soft-Shoe Kick Hops: four times.

12. Toe, heel with the right foot, step on the left foot: eight times. Do not change feet. The toe, heel is done on the right and the step on the left throughout the execution.

13. Repeat Step 3, starting with the right foot.

14. Slap with the right foot, then the left, then the right and the left again.

15. Draw Spring, starting on the right foot. Leave out the heelwork and go into a Grab-Off right and a Grab-Off left.

16. Combination Triples Front and Back: four times. This means four alternating front shuffles and four alternating back shuffles.

17. The Diller: two times, for two complete executions.

18. Swanees: one time, for one complete execution.

19. Buffalo, starting on the right foot: three times, finishing with a step on the right foot and a step on the left foot.

20. Repeat Step 19, shuffling on the left foot.

21. Soft-Shoe steps: four times.

22. Military Basic: four times.

23. The Diller: two times, for two complete executions.

24. Soft-Shoe steps: four times.

25. Military Basic, in a circle: eight times, completing one circle.

26. Draw Spring, using heelwork: one time.

27. River-Boat Shuffle: one time.

28. Soft-Shoe steps: two times.

29. Cross Turn: one time. (*Bow.*)

As you practice this routine you will find how quickly your weight must shift, how all tap tones remain the same without an overly accented beat, and you will soon learn to appreciate the easy grace of the soft-shoe dancer.

Before we go into more advanced tap steps, it would be wise to introduce some more exercises. These exercises will stress footwork, but you should not neglect the body exercises mentioned in earlier chapters. All previously learned exercises should still be practiced periodically along with the new footwork exercises.

Slap exercises are very beneficial and help considerably in building up speed in tap dancing. Merely rise to the balls of your feet and, keeping your feet close to the floor, slap down with your right then left foot, increasing the pace and the tempo of the slaps as you go along.

After a few minutes of this you should do some shuffle exercises. Keeping the feet close to the floor and raising on the half-toe, do a shuffle step alternating the feet each time. Start out slowly and increase your speed. Be sure and keep a 1–2–3 count at all times. It is easy to go so fast that one forgets the count and loses a beat. Next try hop shuffles, again keeping the feet close to the floor. When your speed builds on this exercise you will sound like several galloping horses while doing a hop shuffle, hop shuffle, alternating from the left to right foot.

All of these exercises definitely have their purpose and it is the wise student who never neglects or forgets to include an exercising period before starting her tap lesson.

The tap step called Sevens is a combination of your Threes, or Triples, and Fives, or Waltz Clogs. You are now working at a faster pace and rhythm and body placement come naturally to you. I will not stress arm placement while defining the next steps, for you should by now be able to originate your own arm placement. I would suggest that while learning a new step you keep your hands on your hips until the step is perfected. This helps with balance and still keeps the body nicely postured. Once you have conquered the step, a natural arm placement will come to you. Of course, when doing group work, you or your teacher must set a definite arm placement for each movement so that the group is moving with precision, not only in footwork, but also in body and arm placement.

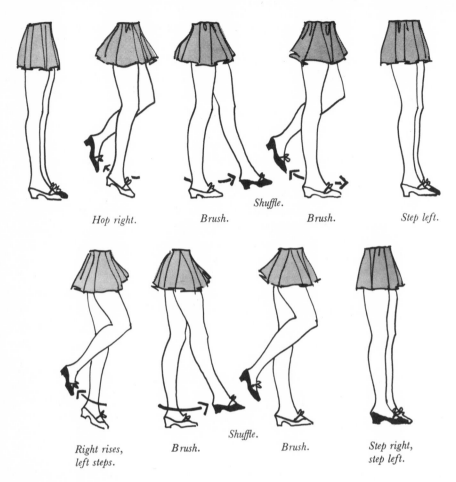

Hop right.   Brush.   Shuffle.   Brush.   Step left.

Right rises,   Brush.   Shuffle.   Brush.   Step right,
left steps.   step left.

28.   Sevens, Step 6.

SEVENS

Sevens are a very important step because they open the
doorway to the more difficult Bucks, and Double Bucks. The
count and the footwork will take thought and time on your
part to perfect but the fun of stepping up to the faster rhythms
will be very enjoyable.

1. Weight is on the left foot.
2. Hop on the left foot.

3. Shuffle step on the right foot, putting weight on the right foot.

4. Shuffle step on the left foot, shifting weight to the left.

5. Step on the right, weight on the right foot.

6. Hop on the right foot and repeat above Steps 3, 4, and 5 with the opposite foot (Fig. 28).

You will note that you hop on the foot that you last stepped on. This must be stressed because it is difficult for the student to remember this. In most dance steps the last foot utilized is not immediately used again. However, in Sevens this does not hold true.

You will also note that I am now using the shuffle term instead of brush-brush. By now your mind quickly grasps this terminology and it is not necessary to stress brush-brush. Your mental picture through Sevens is: hop, shuffle, step; shuffle, step, step and your count is hop, 1–2–3–4–5–6–7. Practice your Sevens until you achieve a continuity of rhythm without accented pauses or beats.

Dances utilizing Sevens may also be used in comedy work. Such routines as "Turkey in the Straw," or "Goofus," may be choreographed with a straw hat, bent knees, and funny body and arm motions bringing forth much appreciation from your audience.

Sevens are usually performed to fast rhythms and therefore it does take some time and practice before you can keep up with the beat of your music. Every tap must ring loud and clear.

To add a bit of variety to your practice the following combination may be used:

1. Sevens, starting the hop on the left foot and shuffling with the right. Do one complete execution.

2. Sevens, starting the hop on the right foot and shuffling with the left. Do one complete execution.

3. Hop, shuffle, step, starting the hop on the left foot and shuffling on the right.

4. Hop, shuffle, step, starting the hop on the right foot and shuffling on the left.

5. Sevens, starting the hop on the left foot. Do one complete execution.

Your mental picture is: hop, shuffle, step, shuffle, step, step; hop, shuffle, step, shuffle, step, step; hop, shuffle, step; hop, shuffle, step, shuffle, step, step.

There are many steps that can be combined in Sevens routines. I shall explain some of the more frequently used ones, but you may put in any of your previously learned steps as long as they suit your music selection.

TRAVELING BUFFALO

In Chapter Three, we discussed Buffalos. By traveling on this step, you can give it a new appearance and add it to your Sevens routine. This should be very easy for you now since you are already able to do the Buffalo correctly in place.

1. Do a Buffalo as previously explained, using Steps 1, 2, and 3.

2. When you are in Step 3, do a step to the right of the stage with the right foot. The step may be large or small.

3. Repeat Step 2, doing a brush-brush on the left foot, moving to the right of the stage with both the shuffle and Step 3 of the previously explained Buffalo, which makes you travel to the right.

I suggest that you cover only a small amount of space in your traveling in the beginning. Should you attempt to cover too great an area, you will lose your nice body placement and your footwork will take on the appearance of a fifty-yard dash.

Another step used often in a Sevens routine is Toe Slides. This is a difficult step to master but time and concentration conquer any step, so do be patient. We usually start a Toe Slide with a shuffle on the foot that we intend to slide. However, for explanation purposes I will not put in the shuffle. You are advanced to the point now that should a shuffle precede a Toe Slide in a routine, you can add it without a detailed explanation.

TOE SLIDES

I will explain this using the right foot. Remember that you must be able to do this equally as well on the left foot.

1. Weight is on the left foot.

29.   Toe Slides, Steps 2 and 3.

2. Place the right foot about six inches in front of the left foot (Fig. 29).

3. Lift the right heel off of the floor and roll the foot over to the right side.

4. Slide the right foot back toward the left foot, with weight still on the left foot.

5. When the right foot is directly in front of the left foot, bring the left foot up and jump over the right foot. The right foot continues to move to the back of the body (Fig. 30) and the left foot has moved about six inches forward from its original place on the floor. Weight is on the left foot.

This is not easy and you must not expect to be able to grasp it immediately. It might be wise to practice this Toe

30. Toe Slides, Step 5.

Slide by placing your palms on the top of a table about waist height. This will help your balance and weight distribution until you master the step. Your mental picture through this step is: slide, jump, without pause or hesitation. It is wise to do a shuffle to bring the right foot back into position to go into another Toe Slide.

The Paddle Turns discussed in soft-shoe dancing can also be very effective in Sevens routines. You execute the same motion as in soft-shoe dancing but you must stay with the music beat of your Sevens routine. You will notice that keeping with a different music beat changes the rhythm of your Paddle Turns.

A very nice turn which was often associated with the late,

great Bill Robinson in his rhythm tap is the Shuffle Spinner. Due to its association with Mr. Robinson many teachers refer to this step by his name. We shall do this without turning in the learning phase and add the turning part after you have learned your position.

SHUFFLE SPINNER

1. Weight is on left foot. Hop on your left foot.
2. Shuffle on the right. (Remember, just a shuffle, no step, this means brush-brush only.)
3. Hop on the left foot, weight still on the left.
4. Slap front on the right foot, weight still on left foot.
5. Hit your toe on the right foot and tap, tap, tap. Pause on the right toe, with weight on your left foot.

Your inner thought is: hop, shuffle, hop, slap, toe, and tap, tap, tap, pause. This simple combination becomes quite difficult as we add the turn, so I suggest that you put some practice into this before attemptimg the following: Using the same combination as above, after Step 3, rise to the ball of the left foot and on the remaining steps pivot the body around to the left, making a complete circle. This must be done smoothly and gracefully.

You are on the ball of the left foot with the weight on the left foot, the right foot helps to pivot the body around to the left. The feet are making their movement close to the floor and the pivoting must be done quickly. Your mental picture remains the same; the only difference is that the body spins around instead of staying in place. Remember to use your spotting in all quick turns.

Numerous shuffle combinations can be used in a Sevens routine and you will probably develop a few of your own as you work on this phase of tap dancing. Interesting footwork is challenging and the following shuffle combination will give you an idea of what changes of foot placement can do to shuffle combinations.

SHUFFLE COMBINATIONS

1. Weight is on the left foot. Shuffle, step on the right foot bringing it in front of the left.

2. Step on the left foot.

3. Shuffle, step again on the right foot and while doing so bring it behind the left.

4. Step on the left foot.

You will note that your weight shifts from right to left very quickly with the left foot holding most of the body weight throughout this combination. Your inner thought is: shuffle step, step, shuffle step, step as your foot moves front and back.

This may also be done by extending one shuffle step far to the right, and the other shuffle step very close to the left foot. Remember to use good arm placement. You also might want to use shuffles to travel forward or backward on the stage, and this can be done by merely doing the shuffle to the front and moving forward on both steps. Reverse the procedure if you should choose to travel to the back of the stage.

STANDARD GRAB-OFF

In Chapter Three we discussed Simple Grab-Offs. You have probably mastered that step completely by now, so the addition of a quick slap and faster motion should come easily to you. The following is the Standard Grab-Off.

1. Follow your pattern of Simple Grab-Off through Step 2.

2. Weight is on the left foot.

3. Shuffle your right foot in front of the left, step on the right toe (ball of foot holding heel off the floor). Weight is shifted quickly to right toe, for at the same time the left foot slaps back on a one count and hits the toe on the other count, the right heel drops to the floor and the weight is on the right foot.

Add a bit of showmanship to this step by extending the left leg far to the back, bending the body from the waist, and crossing the right far in front on the shuffle. Arms extend to the sides in a nice position. Your inner thought through this is: shuffle slap, heel. Actually the feet are doing more than this, but since the left foot and right foot are moving at the same time you cannot mentally count each beat as the feet move.

This must be done very quickly, getting in all of the footwork but moving the feet simultaneously where both the right foot and left foot are doing tap counts throughout parts of the execution.

The following routine will utilize steps learned in this discussion on Sevens and also steps from previous chapters. I suggest you know your material well before attempting the routine.

ROUTINE: "Louisiana Hayride"
4/4 meter time, met beat 170
3 chord, 4-bar introduction
64 bars
1 : 35 minutes

1. Simple Struts: two times.
2. Slap front, right, left, right, left; then repeat Steps 1 and 2.
3. Sevens: two times.
4. Simple Shuffles: eight times, on alternating feet.
5. Runs: four times.
6. Toe Slide: one time.
7. Four Slap Downs, starting right and traveling forward. five times.
8. Cross Turn: one time.
9. Paddle Turns: four times, turning to the left and making a complete circle.
10. Shuffle Spinners: two times.
11. Toe Points to the back: four times, turning to the left and making a complete circle.
12. Grab-Offs, on the right foot: two times.
13. Waltz Clog, stepping on the left foot and shuffling on the right: one time.
14. Military Basic: one time on each foot, starting with the right foot.
15. Repeat Step 13, starting the Waltz Clog step on the right.
16. Repeat Step 14, starting on the left foot.
17. Sevens: four times.
18. Shuffling combinations as explained in this chapter: total of eight times, shuffling on the right and crossing front and back.

19. Simple Struts: two times.

20. Drop heels in place, both right and left simultaneously: two times.

21. Repeat Steps 19 and 20.

22. Slap Backs: four times (r. l. r. l., moving backward).

23. Simple Shuffle steps: eight times.

Repeat, starting with Step 1 and ending with Step 12, using the second Grab-Off as a bow.

Before going any further with this text, it would be wise at this time to treat yourself to a complete review of all the steps and exercises in past chapters. It is so very easy to become involved with new steps and combinations, to the point even where you can neglect to practice previously learned material. You must not allow this to happen. You have no doubt noticed that the steps mentioned in earlier chapters are often included in routines for more advanced work. If you have neglected practicing these steps, you waste valuable time having to relearn the step.

6

Advanced Combinations

WE CAN NOW move on to a series of more difficult steps and combinations, starting with Bucks. These were one time referred to as Buck and Wing Dances, and are a rhythmic tap dancing step which calls for a very controlled body. They are often referred to as a Pick-Up Beat because you start your step on the "and" beat, such as *and* 1–2–3–4.

You have probably watched many great performers do this type of dancing, including Bill Robinson and Donald O'Connor, when using Louis DeProne's choreography. It is also performed by many students who have graduated from the Kent Schools throughout the United States, where rhythm tap or buck dancing is stressed.

You have noted that the flexed knee is necessary in tap dancing and this is especially true with Bucks. In order to accent your rhythm pattern, there will be a definite up and down movement created by coordinated body motion and flexed knees. There are four different main Buck steps and we will start with the Basic, which will prepare you for the Standard, Triple, and Double Bucks. Be sure you have mastered each one before going on to the next.

There are also Standard Buck Breaks, or two-measure movements that usually follow a six-measure time step, which we often call the Buck.

BASIC BUCK

1. Weight is on left foot.
2. Stomp right foot to front.

3. Hop left, keeping weight on the left foot.

4. Slap down to front on the right, shifting weight to the right.

5. Slap down on left, shifting weight to the left.

6. Step right, shifting weight to the right.

7. Repeat, starting stomp on the left foot.

Your thinking through this is: stomp, hop, slap down, slap down, step. Be sure to stay on the balls of your feet through Steps 3, 4, and 5 for a flat-footed dancer does not get the proper ring out of her taps. Also be sure and remember the flexed knees.

STANDARD BUCK

The Standard Buck merely adds a slap, hop to the Basic Buck but you have a completely different sound to your step.

1. Weight on left foot.

2. Stomp right foot to front, keeping weight on left foot.

3. Slap the right foot back to 1 count.

4. Hop on left foot.

5. Slap down to front with right foot, shifting weight to that foot.

6. Slap down to front on left foot, shifting weight to that foot.

7. Step right, shifting weight to right.

8. Repeat, starting stomp on left foot.

Your inner thought now is: stomp, slap, hop, slap down, slap down, step. Remember to keep the feet close to the floor, for it is an ungainly sight to see a Buck performed with feet rising several inches off the floor. All the previously mentioned advice for the Basic Buck also applies to the Standard Buck.

TRIPLE BUCK

The Triple Buck was created by the addition of a shuffle and once again we have another Buck step with an excellent sound.

1. Weight is on the left foot.

2. Stomp right, weight remains on left.

3. Hop left, weight remains on left.

4. Shuffle, step on right, weight shifts to right on step.

5. Slap down on left, shifting weight to left.

6. Step right, shifting weight to right.

7. Repeat, starting stomp with left foot, weight on right.

Your inner thought through the Triple Buck is: stomp, hop, shuffle, step, slap down, step. As mentioned before, the flexed knee, the feet close to the floor, and quick weight shifts add style and develop technique.

DOUBLE BUCK

The Double Buck combines many of the above-mentioned steps and therefore is quite difficult to master. It will take time to develop the proper rhythm and remember all of the combinations, but it is a very rhythmic step and can add much to your dance repertoire.

1. Weight is on left foot.

2. Brush front and back with right to a 1–2 count.

3. Hop left, weight is on left.

4. *Hop again on left.*

5. Shuffle, step right, shifting weight to right.

6. Step left, shifting weight to left.

7. Brush-brush front and back on right.

8. Hop on left, weight is on left.

9. Shuffle, step on right, shifting weight to right.

10. Slap down on left to a 1–2 count, shifting weight to left.

11. Step right.

12. Repeat action, starting with weight on right and brush with left.

You should be thinking: brush-brush, hop, *hop*, shuffle, step, step, brush-brush, hop, shuffle, step, slap down, step. Double Bucks have a continuity of tap beat with no count being over-accentuated or exaggerated. The flexed knee, the foot close to the floor while it executes the tap beat and the loud clear sound of each tap brings forth a rhythmic step that will add class to any rhythm routine.

Bucks can be done in place, in a circle, or traveling in any direction and, by changing stage pattern while doing Bucks, you add variety and interest to your routine. You may utilize steps mentioned before in Buck routines and I will add a few more combinations for your enjoyment.

A break is usually done on the same foot through two executions. There are sometimes exceptions to this rule but not too often.

Buck Break-A.

1. Weight on left foot, right foot stomps, slaps back.
2. Hop on left, weight on left.
3. Slap front step on right, weight quickly shifts to right.
4. Step left.

Repeat entire execution using the same feet, do not alternate.

Buck Break-B (usually used with Double Buck).

1. Weight on left, shuffle on right.
2. Hop on left, keeping weight on left.
3. Slap step to front on right, shifting weight quickly to right.
4. Step left, and shift weight to left.
5. Shuffle right.
6. Hop left, keeping weight on left.
7. Slap step on right, shifting weight to right.
8. Step left.
9. Step right.

You should be thinking: shuffle, hop, slap, step, step, shuffle, hop, slap, step, step, step.

CROSS SPRINGS

Borrowing a step from the ballet world, we have a tap combination that is restful to the dancer and appealing to the audience. This is the *ballet eschappe* referred to as Cross Springs in tap dancing.

1. With weight on both feet, spring out to the half toe on both right and left simultaneously.
2. Knees lock up tightly as right springs to right and left springs to left.
3. Springing again, bring both feet back to original position.

4. Repeat Step 2.

5. Springing again, bring right foot back in front of left, bending knees.

6. Repeat Step 2.

7. Springing again, bring right foot back behind left, bending knees.

Your count is 1–2–3–4–5–6–7–8 and you must be sure to keep your torso straight so that shoulders do not bend with each step.

RHYTHM HEELS

Heel Combinations are always good in Buck routines and here is a new one for you to master. This has a change of rhythm during the execution and a very quick count. By now you have a very flexible ankle so the step should be easy for you to master.

Weight is on left foot.

1. Hop left, weight stays on left.

2. Shuffle heel (heel is on floor and toe points upward) right, quickly shift weight to right heel.

3. Step left.

4. Toe heel (heel on floor, toe points upward) right, weight on right heel.

5. Step left, weight shifts to left.

6. Repeat Step 4.

7. Repeat Step 5.

8. Repeat Step 4 again.

9. Repeat Step 5 again.

Your rhythm change is what adds style to this step. I will accent the rhythm by using italic type for the accented parts of the combination as I explain the mental picture. Toe, heel, step, toe, heel, step, *toe, heel, step, toe, heel, step, toe, heel, step.* As you see your last three *toe, heel, steps* are done loudly and very fast.

MARTHA WASHINGTON

The Martha Washington is a step that can be used in Buck dances or Sevens routines. In fact you will find that this is a very versatile step.

31. Martha Washington, Step 1.   32. Martha Washington, Step 2.

1. Weight is on left foot. Kick, swinging right foot front to the right (Fig. 31).

2. Hop left, both feet off the floor momentarily (Fig. 32).

3. Slap step on right, shifting weight to right, and hop on right. Weight remains on right.

4. Slap back with left, stepping on left, and shifting weight on left.

5. Slap front right, stepping on right, and shifting weight to right.

6. Chug front on right only, bringing left toe (in a turned-down position) into position near right ankle with a turned-out knee (Fig. 33).

7. Step on left, shifting weight to left.

33. Martha Washington, Step 6.

You should be thinking: kick, hop, slap back, hop, slap
back, slap front, chug, step. Although almost all of these
explanations are given with the right foot performing most
of the action, it is up to you to perfect every step alternating
feet and developing the left foot as much as the right.

The old-fashioned Charleston step, along with Ball-of-
Foot Struts, can be combined to add rest in your Buck
dancing and still keep a nice style. In fact any of your previous struts may be used as long as you keep the beat of your
music. The following routines combine many of your previously learned steps with steps and combinations presented
in this chapter. I would suggest that you memorize your
step pattern before attempting the routines to music. Once

you can go smoothly from one step to another, it is then time to attempt the routine to the suggested music.

ROUTINE: "Winter Wonderland"
          4/4 meter time, met beat 144
          3 chord, 4-bar introduction
          64 bars
          1 : 35 minutes

1. Sevens: four times.
2. Run: one time.
3. Simple Struts, forward: four times.
4. Grab-Off, turning half way to the right, finishing with Brush-Brush, Step on left; step right, turning body in a half circle with your back to the audience.
5. Repeat Step 4, turning to finish the circle and face audience.
6. Sevens: two times.
7. Simple Struts: four times.
8. Buffalos traveling to left, finishing with slap down right, step left, step right; repeat, starting slap with left foot: two times on each foot.
9. Rock: one time.
10. Ball-of-Foot Strut, to count of 8: one time.
11. Paddle Turns to count of 8.
12. Hop on left, shuffle right, hop on left, shuffle right, hop on left, shuffle right, and go into Grab-Off on right.
13. Repeat Step 12, using hop on right, shuffle on left, and Grab-Off on left.
14. Heel Drops: four times (r. l. r. l.).
15. Pull Backs: 3 steps on 4th count on left.
16. Shuffle Spinner: one time.
17. Martha Washington: one time.
18. Buffalos to right, finishing with slap downs as explained in Step 8: two times.
19. Shuffle Spinner: one time.
20. Shuffle Combinations: Shuffle step right, crossing in front of left. Shuffle step left, crossing in front of right. Shuffle step right not crossing, shuffle step left not crossing, shuffle step right, shuffle step left, step right. You might think

"What's the time, what's the time, tell me please what is the time," through this combination in order to get your rhythm. Do this combination two times.

21. Sevens: two times.

22. Toe Points, making a complete circle to count of 8.

23. On right, weight on left, brush-brush, hop left, extend toe to back and hit toe of right. Do twice. Mental picture is: brush-brush hop toe.

24. Slap down, step, step forward starting on right.

25. Slap down, step, step forward on left.

26. Repeat Steps 24, 25, turning right side to audience.

27. Slaps starting on right to right, left side now to audience: four times.

28. Scoot Backs, left side to audience: two times.

29. One Cross Turn and tap, tap, tap, facing audience at completion.

30. Brush-brush on right, hop left, repeat, step left. Mental picture: brush-brush, hop, brush-brush, hop, step.

31. Martha Washington.

32. Kick left, hop right, kick left, hop right, step left. Mental picture: kick hop, kick hop, step.

33. Sevens: two times.

34. Grab-Off, right.

35. Grab-Off, left. Onto knee from Grab-Off for bow.

ROUTINE: "Dark Town Strutters Ball"
4/4 meter time, met beat 152
3 chord, 4-bar introduction
64 bars
1 : 48 minutes

1. Standard Buck: six times.

2. Buck Break-A: two times.

3. Buffalos, three to Grab-Off, traveling to right.

4. Repeat Step 3 combination, traveling to left.

5. Standard Buck: two times.

6. Starting on right, brush-brush hop: total of four times (r. l. r. l.).

7. Paddle Turns turning to right to count of 7, with a step making the 8th count.

8. Triple Buck: four times.

9. One Toe Slide, finishing with slap down, step, step right; slap down, step, step left.

10. Cross Springs: one complete execution.

11. Triple Buck: four times.

12. Simple Charleston, step, right and left.

13. Simple Struts, forward: four times.

14. Rhythm Heels Combination: two times.

15. Double Buck: four times.

16. Brush-brush, right, hop left, slap down right, step left. Repeat, alternating feet: total of four times.

17. Grab-Offs in a circle: four times, to make complete circle turning to left.

18. Sevens: two times.

19. Swanees as explained on page 97, remembering to keep with rhythm: total of eight times.

20. Double Bucks: two times.

21. Cross Turn for bow.

Routines are much easier for you to read and remember now and as you read the step your mind should grasp the action and count. You will find that as your work becomes more difficult you understand your subject more thoroughly, and through your dedicated practice you have progressed into some difficult tap dancing steps.

The ones I will explain to you now will not be accomplished quickly. They are very difficult and require much time and control. They will be a real challenge to you but, when conquered, will make you feel completely satisfied with your endeavours and accomplishments. There are several different types of Wings and all of them are difficult. They require concentration with much practice, and tremendous body coordination. Naturally, they are very showy and are a must for all dancers.

DOUBLE WINGS

We shall start with the Double Wing. Perhaps it is the most difficult to execute, but it does develop the style and technique which make the other wings seem much easier. I would suggest that you start your practice of Double Wings using a table top for support. Face the table and put both hands on the table top. Through the learning stage, your hands can carry your weight and assist with balance.

1. Weight is on both feet.

2. The knees flex almost to a bend.

3. Using the table to assist with weight distribution and balance, push your right foot to the right, left foot to the left, doing a shuffle on both feet at the same time. Come back into starting position with a step on both feet at the same time, weight shifting to even distribution on both feet. This is done very quickly and weight remains on the balls of the feet throughout the entire execution. The knees remain flexed; they cannot tighten. Keep shoulders pulled back and chin up.

In time when you are able to do Double Wings without the assistance of the table top, you may let your arms make a circular motion moving inward in the beginning of the circular motion and then out, right arm going to the right, left going to the left, reaching above the head and back (to the beginning position.) This arm motion also helps with balance, but it will take some time before you are able to coordinate body, feet, and arms.

After mastering the Double Wings the following wings will be much easier to master. If you wish to use the table top through the learning phase do so: however, many of you will be able to go through these wings without too much difficulty, for the Double Wings have helped to prepare you for the following:

SINGLE WINGS

1. For explanation purposes we will use the right foot. Weight is on right foot.

2. Left leg is held behind right foot about ankle height.

3. The left foot does not touch the floor through a Single Wing.

4. Flex right knee, rise to the ball of the foot and push right foot to the right, executing a shuffle step on right only.

5. Repeat complete action without changing feet.

Again for explanation purposes I will use the right foot. This wing is very similar to the Single Wing, the only exception being that the left leg swings front and back, like the pendulum of a clock, making a tap sound with the toe as it passes from front to back and vice versa.

1. Weight is on the right foot.

2. Left foot is off the floor.

3. Flex the right knee, rise to the ball of the foot and push your right foot to the right, executing a shuffle step on right.

4. At the same time you are doing Step 3, swing your left leg to the front tapping the floor with your toe as the leg goes through this motion. Repeat Single Wing and swing left leg to back, tapping floor with toe as leg passes to the back.

Be sure and keep a nice body posture while doing wings. With shoulders drooping or leaning forward, with head down and arms dangling, the difficulty of the step you are performing is completely lost to your viewers due to the grotesque appearance of your body.

FALLING OFF THE LOG

Falling off the Log is a combination of shuffles, cross steps, and rhythm change. The step itself is not too difficult, but the high kicks and the body position throughout the step take some time to perfect.

The step itself is self-explanatory. Actually, one must feel as though one is really trying to keep from falling off a moving log. The body leans with the step motion and the kicks are quick and high.

1. Weight is on the left foot.

2. Hop on the left foot.

3. Shuffle step on the right foot behind the left, shifting weight to right on step and also on step left rises high toward the right.

4. Step down on the left foot to left, turning your body to the left and shifting weight to the left.

5. Cross the right foot over in front of the left, shifting your

body with the action, and step on the right foot shifting weight to the right.

6. Step on the left foot directly behind the right shifting weight to the left.

7. Step down on the right foot behind the left, shifting weight to the right and raising the left foot high and toward the right of the body.

8. Step down on the left foot, placing it next to the right and shift weight to the left.

9. Step down on the right foot crossing in front of the left, shifting weight to the right foot and raising the left foot behind the right near calf height.

Much body motion must go into this step and as you perfect the foot movements keep a mental picture of falling and trying to retain balance. Actually, your thinking through this is: hop, shuffle, kick, step, cross, step, back, step, front. This describes the action of the right foot.

BELLS

Bells are actually a clicking of the heels together while the body is suspended in the air. There are many ways to go into Bells and every teacher has her favorite combination. One must reach height or give an illusion of elevation while doing this step. Those of you who have a natural talent for jumping will probably choose this as one of your favorite steps. Others who do not have this special talent will have to give an illusion of elevation with body motion.

1. Weight is on the left foot.

2. Hop on the left foot.

3. Shuffle step on the right foot shifting weight to the right on the step.

4. As you step on the right foot raise your left leg to right calf height.

5. Step down on the left foot next to the right foot, shifting weight to left.

6. Step down on the right foot crossing it in front of the left, shifting weight to the right.

7. Extend left foot to the left, high off the floor, in a locked position with toe pointed toward the left.

8. Flex the knee of the right leg and spring off the floor, bringing the right foot up to the left foot and hitting the heels together.

Be sure you bring the foot which is on the floor up to the extended foot. It is very easy to lower the height of the extended foot and bring it down to the rising foot. This loses all the smart appearance of this step. You will find as you practice and your body muscles become more elastic, your kicking height will increase considerably.

AIR TURNS

This particular step is used in all types of dancing, whether it be tap, ballet, or jazz. It is very effective when done with a minimum of tapping but a lot of body motion. It must be executed quickly and with perfect body control.

1. Feet are side by side and weight is on both feet.
2. Bend both knees.
3. Using your right shoulder to give a push, spring high into the air, making the body turn in one complete circle before landing.
4. Land quietly on both feet with knees flexed.

In the beginning, in all probability, you will only make half a turn. Determination and practice will soon advance you to the stage where a complete turn is very easy and you will attempt making two complete turns in the air before landing.

COSSACKS

This combination is from Russian folk dancing; it is very difficult, requiring perfect balance and coordination. The body position alone is hard to maintain without the addition of the leg kicks. I suggest you learn this step by grasping two stationary objects, such as chairs or tables, with your right and left hands. These objects must be placed at the right and left sides of the body, for the front space must be clear for the kicks.

1. Sink into a squatting position. Feet are side by side and weight at this time is on the balls of both feet.
2. Heels are raised.

34. Cossacks, Step 4.

3. Shift weight to the ball of the left foot.

4. With a spring hop on the left you push the right heel to the front, the right leg is forward and straight, and the toe is pointed, the right heel hits the floor (Fig. 34).

5. As you pull the right leg in to the starting position shift weight from the ball of the left foot to the ball of the right foot; the left leg extends forward and the foot positions are reversed.

6. There is a bouncy spring with each extension and the thigh is firm and tight, for it is carrying most of the weight of the upper torso.

Your count is 1 and; 2 and; 3 and; 4. On 1 you are springing and extending, while on *and* you are hitting the heel. This is also true with your 2 *and* count, but with the opposite foot. The proper hand placement for this is crossed-arm position, chest high, held firmly in front of the body.

Cossacks are very showy and receive much acclaim, they are also very difficult and must be practiced diligently for many weeks before they can be done properly.

Variations of Cossacks are easy to do once you have mastered the original step. They are also very showy and add much to your skill. By using an up-and-down body motion, a very spectacular movement can be added to your routine. Complete the full 8 count of your Cossack, return to beginning position with weight on the balls of both feet and in squatting position; spring up to full body height, shifting weight to the right foot with left heel extended to the left side, toe up. Sink back into squatting position, extending your right heel to the right with toe up. The heel is on the floor. Your body is going through an up-and-down motion, from a squat to full height in a quick 1 and 2 count, sinking on 3, and rising again with heel hitting floor on the 4 count. As you see, this is a very quick count to perform such complete changes of body position. This is a challenging step but well worth mastering.

COFFEE GRINDERS

Again we are in a squatting position with both hands in front on the floor.

1. Weight is on the ball of the left foot.

2. The right leg is extended straight and to the right, with the heel on the floor and the toe up and pointed.

3. The right leg swings front and to the left, remaining stiff throughout the entire movement.

4. As the right leg passes the position of the right hand, the right hand rises over the passing leg and takes a position on the floor to the right of the right leg, and weight now shifts to the *right hand*.

5. The left hand now passes over the right leg, which is held stiff and is moving toward the left.

6. Weight is only on the right hand; the left hand is on the floor, free to assist balance.

35. Coffee Grinders, Step 7.

7. The right leg now moves in front of the left foot (Fig. 35).

8. The left foot rises up and over the extended right leg at thigh position.

9. The right leg continues on its circle behind the body and back to its starting position (Fig. 36).

The stiffly extended right leg is actually making a complete circle; obstacles, such as the hands and left foot, pass over this leg as it reaches their respective positions. The torso is held straight and stiff and the chin is up throughout this step. A sloppy body position and a bent right knee ruin the visual effect of a Coffee Grinder and send teachers and audience into complete frustration. Do not include Coffee Grinders in any routine until you are doing them properly and

36.   Coffee Grinders, Step 9.

with flair and style. One Coffee Grinder should be completed
in a 1–2 count, and this is quite speedy for such a difficult
step. You can appreciate the many hours of practice and
perfection the next time you watch a dancer perform a Coffee
Grinder.

The following routine contains many of these advanced
steps. Do not attempt it to the suggested music until you
have mastered the continuity of the choreography and are
able to go from one step to another without pause or hesitation.

ROUTINE: "The Marine Hymn"
              2/4 meter time, met beat 204
              3 chord, 4-bar introduction
              2 choruses
              64 bars

1. Standard Buck: six times.
2. Buck Break-A: two times.
3. Repeat Steps 1 and 2.
4. Falling off the Log: two times.
5. Grab-Off, traveling forward: four times.
6. Triple Buck: three times.
7. Toe Slide: two times.
8. Double Buck: two times.
9. Toe heel right, step left: four times.
10. Cossacks: four times.
11. Cossack variations: four times.
12. One Run, Cross Turn, and into Air Turns: one time.
13. Bells: two times.
14. Shuffle step: four times (r. l. r. l.).
15. Double Wings: two times.
16. Single Wings: two times.
17. Pendulum Wings: two times.
18. Grab-Off. (*Bow.*)

The preceding text has brought you from the very beginning basics through to the advanced steps. If you have practiced and studied as you should, you are no doubt now making up combinations of your own by adding a heel step or a shuffle, or even a toe slide. Your coordinated arm motions assist with your balance and add a finished touch to your performance. You have mastered quick weight shifts, along with flexed knee and ball of foot positions. In fact, you are probably even designing some of your own routines. Time, patience, and practice have helped you to become a polished performer and dancer. Now you need some ideas on variety of presentation.

7

Novelty
Tap Dancing

VARIETY is the spice of life and this is certainly true with dancing. Different presentations appeal to the dancer as well as the audience, and clever novelty work in any program or performance keeps the audience very interested and the dancers enthused. These two ingredients spell success for teacher and student alike. Costuming and music go hand in hand with novelty work. We will spend more time in a later chapter on a discussion of costuming, but it will be mentioned briefly here.

Any type of Western presentation is usually always welcomed by your viewers. This could be boys or girls in Western gear using lassos or guns throughout their performance. Indian costuming, with the dancers using bows and arrows or tomtoms, is also appealing and usually receives a spontaneous burst of applause.

Always a show stopper is a comedy barnyard or farm scene which can be created in many ways. Using two students in a horse's body, which can be rented from a theatrical supply house, is a good comedy number when set to the tune of "The Old Gray Mare." An advanced dancer, dressed in some type of farm costume, can highlight the show with a dance performed from the floor onto a milking stool and back to the floor. This takes some planning because the steps to be done on the milking stool must be adapted to the size of the stool. Also, too heavy a jump will tilt the stool, causing the dancer to take an unplanned spill. One can

132

understand why this should be undertaken only by a more advanced student.

A very dainty novelty number in keeping with the farm theme can be done by having little girls dressed as milk maids carrying buckets and stools with the props used through mime motions during different parts of the dance.

Be sure that appropriate background music is included when designing a novelty routine. For instance, to the tune of "Goofus," one should add exaggerated body motions, long leg pulls, high hops, and droopy arm motions to create the desired effect.

Waltz Clogs are very adaptable to novelty dancing. In a previous chapter I mentioned the jump rope and stair dances that utilize this step. When the dancer wears roller skates and is performing to "The Skaters' Waltz" the Waltz Clog can again be used. This is a fairly easy step to perform on roller skates and the dance can actually include some very nice skating to this tune. Balance is essential, but a good dancer and skater should have no trouble performing it.

To the melody of "Take Me Out to the Ball Game" it is possible to use costumed dancers in baseball hats and uniforms who actually perform a ball game through mime and Waltz Clog steps. The pitcher pitches, the batter strikes and dances from base to base as the catcher, basemen, and umpire go through all the movements of the ball game while performing a Waltz Clog routine. This idea goes over very well with the audience and makes a clever production number.

"Me and My Shadow" is an old standard in the novelty dance field, and you have no doubt seen it performed on television and in movies. It is always a crowd pleaser but it takes much time to perfect. Two dancers, one a bit shorter than the other, must perform as one, typifying the theme of "Me and My Shadow." The shadow is costumed in black and through stage lighting can take on the appearance of a real shadow. Because of the precision movements required of the two performers, it is wise to choose two students of equal training and ability.

Umbrellas added to any novelty number are appealing.

They also allow dancers to catch a breath through the routine as umbrellas spin or sway gracefully to the music. Soft-shoe dancing is best suited for umbrella work, because the music is slower and one has more time to work-in the umbrella movements.

Of course, the old standard top hat and cane are always a welcome sight and many clever cane and hat motions can be added to the choreography of a routine. One usually pictures Bucks or Rhythm Taps with these props.

The student with advanced skills and talents can do much when it comes to presenting novelty work. The child who has reached the toe-dancing stage in ballet greatly pleases the audience when she presents a toe tap. Taps designed for toe shoes are placed on the toe shoe and any type of dance, whether it be a Buck, Waltz Clog, or Sevens is eyecatching. This is difficult work and you will find that many steps which require a great deal of leaning do not lend themselves to toe-tap dancing.

The baton twirler, doing a very fast military tap dance while also going through intricate baton twirls, can easily be the hit of the show if all motions are coordinated and performed with smooth continuity.

The Swiss Flag Swinger can move gracefully through a soft-shoe dance using the lovely flowing motions of the Swiss Flag throughout the routine. The student of acrobatics, who can go quickly from Wings into a split, from a Buck Break into a handspring, or who can adroitly dip into a back bend while doing a Soft Shoe, has no difficulty when called upon to present something which is different.

The Samoan Sword Spinner, going through difficult sword movements while performing a Rhythm Tap to percussion or bongo drums or even a lilting Polynesian melody, will be rewarded with a tremendous ovation at the completion of the number.

Props, music, and costuming add much when it comes to novelty dancing. However, one can do a great deal with lighting and the fluorescent or strobe light can certainly be used to advantage. This light can be purchased or rented from a theatrical supply house. It is blue in color and when other stage lights are dimmed or turned off, the strobe light picks up the color of the fluorescent materials used in this type of costuming, thus giving the effect of beautiful neon lighting. Remember, though, if you plan to use the strobe light all materials or paint used in the numbers must be fluorescent. There is a wealth of ideas when it comes to using the strobe light. The following are only a few sketches that will start your own mind working.

Kids in the Three-cornered Pants: This is a tiny tot number performed to the song with the same title. The children are dressed in a cleverly designed plain satin costume that is not of fluorescent material. However, on the tights use fluorescent sequins and outline the shape of a diaper in front with a huge safety pin done in the sequins.

It is a good idea to have a vocalist sing this number, for someone must recite the words to the music as the children dance. Each time the song comes to the words "It's nobody else but the kids in their three-cornerd pants," the dancers take a quick turn, face the audience, daintily raise their skirts, point their toes, hold this position, and the stage lights go out, the strobe light comes on and the sequins light up in the shape of a pinned diaper!

Following a slight pause, the stage lights come on again and the dancers continue with their routine until it is time to repeat the words "It's nobody else but the kids in the three-cornered pants." I used this particular number in a large recital in California and it was very well received.

Dry Bones: This is a wonderful routine for a Halloween show, but can be used at other times, too. To the music of the same name, a comedy dance is designed which uses many arm motions, hops, and stage movements. Using a black leotard and tights, and a black scarf for a face covering, paint the form of a skeleton in white fluorescent paint on the black surface. The entire number is done with stage lights out and the strobe light on. The eerie appearance of dancing skeletons will delight your audience.

Tiptoe Through the Tulips: This is a very beautiful number which can be done in a variety of ways. Fluorescent tulips on the backdrop with floral tulip costuming is pretty, or one can use the previously mentioned umbrellas covered in a fluorescent tulip design with plain costumes. The effect of the spinning flowers on the umbrellas is equally as attractive as the costume and backdrop combination. One can even paint a jump rope in fluorescent paint which matches or blends with the costume, and this can also be very effective.

The preceding examples are just a few ways in which fluorescent paints and materials can be utilized. When using them, however, remember that the dancers' movements must be very precise, because the strobe light will highlight every mistake.

Other ideas for novelty dance routines can often be derived from the area in which you live. In Japan, we used Japanese fans while performing to the "Japanese Sandman," while in England we developed a routine based on the game of darts and performed to the tune of "Penny a Pitch." Our foreign hosts very much enjoyed each presentation.

By using a bit of imagination and creativity, there is a great deal you can do in the field of novelty dancing. Ideas may come to you at times when you are not even working on novelty routines, which you can jot down and file away for future reference. To make any performance more exciting and to give your audience a special treat, make sure you include one or two novelty numbers in each show.

8

Helpful Hints on Costuming

AS YOU KNOW by now, background music adds much to a dancer's routine, but another ingredient must be added to complete the picture. That, of course, is costuming. One could write an entire volume on costuming. There is so much to be said on this subject and each person or teacher will run into individual problems which only experience and time will solve.

All costume materials should be purchased at a theatrical supply store. Granted, you can buy satins and velvets at department stores but they do not have the available choices and combinations of theatrical materials. You will find numerous designs and prints in all sorts of materials at a theatrical supply house. If you do not live close to any of these suppliers, you can send for their catalogues and in each catalogue there are sample swatches of the materials along with width and price lists. Listed on page 175 are the names of several supply houses which have excellent yearly catalogues for you.

Buckram headdresses that only have to be covered, marabou fur, plain and fluorescent sequins, in fact everything you will need is in the catalogues. Of course, whenever possible it is wise to go in person to the supplier. Then you can see first hand the many selections which they have to offer. If this is not feasible, however, your entire recital can be costumed through mail order.

There is much to be taken into consideration when planning costumes, cost and design being two of the most important factors. Should you be costuming a group of dancers who plan many performances, the design of the costume should be such that different sequins, fringe, or overskirts can be added to change the appearance of the costume. Also, all figure flaws should be disguised in costume design. The children with thin arms should have full net, nylon, or satin sleeves. The child with a protruding tummy does not look her best in a tight-fitting leotard design, while a very narrow torso needs fullness rather than a snug fit.

Costs of costuming should be kept at a minimum. With planning and imagination you can design and choose very showy material for student costuming at a minimum cost.

However, there are also times when a very elegant costume is needed and desired by student and parent. This should be discussed beforehand and agreed upon by all individuals involved; then watching pennies will not be necessary.

Always take parents into consideration when planning costumes. After all, they are picking up the tab, and since a variety of costumes are required for most dance students, you can shatter the family economy if you are not prudent and practical.

Most materials at theatrical supply houses are 42 or 44 inches in width and this is good to know when making several costumes of the same design out of the same material.

The beautiful shine of perma-jewels, the combinations of metallic silver and fuchsia, the lamé and sequin cloth are only a few that make showy and elegant-looking costumes at a minimum cost. As you browse through your theatrical catalogue you will be amazed at the attractive materials offered at low prices.

In many numbers the choice of material design depends solely on the dance number. Several costume suggestions are shown on the following pages. For instance when your group or you are performing the Irish Jig, the costume must blend with the number. White satin with huge green shamrocks can be found in most catalogues and this material done up in full short skirt, sweetheart neckline, and short full puff sleeves with a wide green cumberbund can be adorable.

37. Costume suggestions for Irish Jig and military numbers.

38. Costumes using fluorescent materials.

Also solid green with shamrocks on wrist cuffs, headdress, and shoe ties could be used satisfactorily.

It would be unthinkable to put your Irish Jig number on stage without appropriate costumes to blend with the theme. The same is true with military numbers. The costumes should definitely have some type of military design and, of course, all fluorescent numbers must have fluorescent materials.

Comfortable tights are a must, and with younger students the bloomer tight is most satisfactory. These are easy to make, do not bind or feel tight during a performance, and can be worn for sometime as small bodies change and develop. Many of my older students prefer the bloomer tight over the more fitted tight. Regardless of the type of tights chosen to wear under a costume, however, they must be comfortable and allow freedom of motion.

There must be some type of headdress with each costume, and this too must be chosen wisely. The tiny tots cannot wear a large headdress. Their hair is usually not thick enough to firmly hold a huge headdress and just the added weight of this interferes with their dancing.

39.　Costumes using feathers and fur.

There are many designs of headdresses from tiaras to ribbons. Buckram frames can be ordered and covered by matching costume material, which is very easy to do . Merely cut your material to the size of the headdress and, using an instant-drying adhesive, glue the material onto the buckram. If you are on a limited budget you may cut your headdress designs out of cardboard and glue the material over this. The headdress must blend with the costume design and dance number and, most importantly, it must fit securely on the head. Nothing is more exasperating to a dancer than trying to perform with the worry of the headdress falling off.

Many times feathers can be used very effectively as a head-dress; also bands of marabou fur; if marabou is used as a costume trim, make an attractive and easy to wear design. Ordinary bicycle clips with ruffled material slipped over them fit securely and are most attractive, too.

The high top-hat frames can be ordered in black felt, or in buckram frames, and covered. These can also be used for that fancy number in solid sequins which glitter like millions of bright stars on the stage. Top hats can always be sized by running a roll of sheeting around the inside brim, should you

40. Other costume suggestions.

find that your students' heads simply do not measure out enough to wear the hat. We have even on one occasion, when the hats arrived about one hour before the show went on, stuffed the insides with newspaper to fill them up and give a secure fit.

I am a firm believer in using a small rolled or narrow flesh-colored elastic band attached to the headdress, which is slipped under the chin and behind the ears of the dancer to hold the headdress in place. Bobby pins can be used but they sometimes slip out of place; the elastic band really keeps the headdress in permanent postion. The headdress is very important in creating a finished picture, but it must be designed properly and fit securely in order to give the dancer a comfortable feeling while performing.

Whenever several students are performing in one number and you want all costumes to be identical, it is wise to hire a seamstress to do each costume. This assures you of uniformity in the finished product. It is easy for parents to misunderstand a design and oftentimes, unless one individual makes all costumes, you will find yourself feeling very frustrated at dress rehearsal, when you see fringe or sequins going a different direction on each costume.

Shoes should also be dressed up in some manner and there are many ways to do this. Merely by adding a colored ribbon to the tap shoe, a ribbon that will blend in with costume and headdress, you bring the design down to the feet. Also, glitter in any color can be placed over the shoes. This is done by first putting masking tape over the entire area you wish to glitter, usually the entire shoe. Then using the instant-drying adhesive, smear the adhesive over the masking tape. Sprinkle on the glitter, which sticks instantly. Once the performance is over strip off the masking tape, and the shoe is once again back to normal. Gold and silver glitter pick up stage lighting beautifully. However, if you wish to use a glitter that matches the costume, do so for this, too, adds much to the overall appearance of the dancer.

All different colors of paints are also available for the shoe. Silver, gold, pastels, or bright solid colors can be used. I am a firm believer in the masking-tape method, for once the shoe

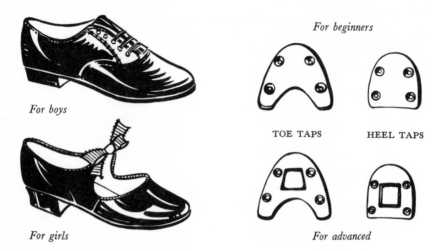

For boys

For girls

For beginners

TOE TAPS   HEEL TAPS

For advanced

41.   Tap shoes and taps.

is painted or glittered it takes quite some time for this to wear off and many times your dancer wishes to wear a different color shoe before the old color or glitter has completely disappeared. When using the masking tape it is very simple to remove the tape and bring the shoe back to normal right after the performance.

Fluorescent paints can also be used on the shoes and this looks lovely under strobe lights. When using fluorescent paint, however, I do not advise you to cover the entire shoe. I did this on one occasion many years ago and was appalled when my dancers feet took on the appearance of "Minnie Mouse" under the light. Now I merely stripe the shoe in fluorescent paint. Usually this is about an inch stripe starting at the sole and going completely around the shoe. Oftentimes I will use a fluorescent ribbon on the tap shoe along with the striping, which gives just the right effect and draws attention to the footwork.

Arms must not be neglected either. Many costumes will have a long-sleeved or puff-sleeved design. Those without sleeves must have the finished touch of gauntlets or cuffs. Gauntlets fit snugly up the arm, sometimes to the elbow, and are held on with an elasticized thread over the middle

42. Suggestions for gauntlets and cuffs.

finger or wrist. Gauntlets have numerous designs, with some starting at the wrist and others going to a point over the top of the hand. They can be made of net, or the same type of materials used in your costumes. The pictures and sketches of gauntlets will help you to realize the different designs, and your catalogues from the theatrical supply house also have many styles to choose from.

Cuffs, usually about four to six inches in height, fit around the wrists, are backed by heavy buckram or cardboard, and fit snugly in place through elastic with, if extra long, the addition of hooks and eyes. The backing must be covered with the same material as your costume and trimmed in the same type of trim that you have used on your costume.

Imitation floral sprays can also be used as wrist wear in dance numbers and there are a variety of these featured in the catalogues. Small children can manage with a large bow tied on the wrists if it fits in with the costume design, and your older students can wear a feather arrangement when suitable.

Cuffs can be made in a heart design, diamond design, shamrock design, or even just a square or round shape. This is decided by the number you or your group are doing and the design of your costume.

Every piece of costume from shoes, tights, cuffs, or gauntlets, should have your name or your student's name in it. Decide beforehand just where you want the name placed on each garment and see to it that the student remembers to do this. This saves much time and confusion in the dressing room before and after programs when all costumes are alike and are almost identical in size. A small piece of adhesive tape can be placed inconspicuously on costume and accessories with the student's name written in ink. First and last name should be used when space permits. If the area is small, such as on cuffs or a narrow headdress, all three initials or some type of identifying mark should be legible to identify all the Lindas, Pams, or Susies you might have in the particular number.

The child or his parents must pay for all the cost of costuming, and it is the wise teacher who remembers to include the cost of thread, trim, elastic, and all needed materials. When a dressmaker is used, this cost is also absorbed by student or parent and, to save time for everyone concerned, all costs should be included when you send sketches of the costume to be used to parent or student. Include where it will be made, dates of fittings, and the total cost for each individual. It is also the wise teacher who keeps a record of the individual cost should there be questions about it at a later date. Small cards of snaps or hooks and eyes sound incidental to you when you think of ordering. However, if there are many dancers performing in the number, you will find that unless you have remembered to include these items in your initial cost statement to parents, you must pay for them yourself and this can cut quite deeply into your profits. Elastic for tights for one person is not costly, but multiply it by twenty or thirty and you will see that it does amount up to a tidy sum.

Thre are many places where one can order ready-made costumes and these are very showy and quite elegant. They are made of elasticized stretch materials in most cases, and one size fits almost any body shape in that size. The trim, arm dress, and headdress come as a package deal and eliminate the need for a dressmaker. I find that these are a bit more costly than the costumes designed and made for each individual student but they do have some advantages. They save quite a bit of time you would ordinarily spend with scheduling fittings and trips to the theatrical supply house, or waiting for materials to arrive by mail in order to get them to the dressmaker. But they also have some disadvantages, too.

Many times you cannot find a costume that fits the dance numbers you are doing. Also I have found that there is a certain sameness about the leotard cut of each one. I rarely use ready-made costumes. It is much more satisfying to create the design, choose the material, and trim the costumes in the brilliant color combinations that I want. This gives me a feeling of fulfillment and I thoroughly enjoy designing and browsing through theatrical houses or catalogues until I find just the right materials. However, many of my teacher friends use ready-made costumes exclusively and find them very satisfactory.

Regardless of what type of costume and accessories you choose, the finished product must be treated with care. It is part of your dance wardrobe and should be kept along with all accessories in a garment bag, or plastic covering. It should be placed properly on its hanger with accessories pinned onto an accompanying hanger. The costume should be cleaned and pressed periodically to keep it fresh and should be repaired whenever necessary. Fringe can slip, sequins can become loose, hooks and eyes through strain will need new stitching and this should be done immediately when necessary and not put off until a couple of minutes before the next performance.

High hats should be in a hat box or draw-string cloth-covered bag. They should not be just laid on the closet shelf where dust can accumulate and dim their nice satin shine or sequin sparkle. Shoes must be polished, reglittered, or repainted when they need to be. In other words, your entire dance wardrobe should always be in first-class shape.

The snappiest dance, with classic choreography, will look like nothing if the performers' costumes are in a natty condition. The illustrations in this chapter will give you some idea on costuming and accessories. You might adopt some of these for your own routines but in all probability you are eager to start working on your own costume and accessory designs. Remember to keep your costs in mind, flatter your figure with your costume design, care for the costume lovingly, and wear it with pride.

9

On Stage: Programs, Workshops, and the Big Recital

PERFORMING before an audience is a must for the dancer. Through stage performance the student acquires confidence, learns about showmanship, thrills to audience applause, and develops poise, all of which help to develop a good entertainer. Taking part in programs is a necessity for the dance student, and every teacher should see to it that all of her students have opportunities to perform throughout their terms of study.

There are many places where dancers are welcomed whole-heartedly by program chairmen. The schools, PTA's, Girls Scouts, plus many community organizations will be very eager to include a dancer in their many programs. Talent shows throughout your area need your ability and in numerous places television stations have shows where the amateur is able to appear on a competitive basis, thus giving one an inside view of what is expected of the professional dancer.

Dance schools and teachers also put on their own programs and I suggest that before the "big recital," which is usually held at the end of the term, the students be subjected to at least one workshop recital. If your students have never had an opportunity to perform, often a workshop recital is a necessity. This is a very informal program, where costuming might be just the practice clothing. It is open to all parents and friends, and sometimes the teacher even invites the general public. A workshop recital lacks the glamour of the

148

big yearly recital. There is a very relaxed attitude and the entire evening stresses informality. Through a workshop recital the teacher might even explain her method of teaching to interested parents.

A coffee hour after the program is a good time for conversation and questions. Although informal, the workshop recital is very beneficial to the student. For many young children this is their first appearance on stage, and to them the thrill of the moment is as big as if they were appearing on the stage of Radio City Music Hall. This performance prepares the student for future programs and also the big recital where extravagance prevails.

Workshop recitals may be held in the studio or at some rented auditorium. They do not require the many months of planning that the yearly recital must have. When working with several hundred students, I have used a workshop as the time to present student awards. This eliminates added time from the big recital when one has a a large class enrollment.

Even this type of recital requires some advanced planning. Of course the dance numbers or the exercises that the students will be doing must be practiced beforehand so the students can perform to perfection. Dressing rooms should be checked beforehand and at least one rehearsal should be held. All of the area should be checked completely. Lavatories should be located and each student told of their whereabouts. One does not have to go to great lengths concerning lighting and backdrop decorations in a workshop; however, out of respect to your students and your audience, there should be some token effort made in this direction.

Regardless of where my students are performing, there are certain standard measures that I put into effect. Often I ask parents and friends to bring flashlights to the performances, and then station these people backstage and in the audience. In case of an unexpected power failure, bedlam does not reign as many little people become frightened trying to find their way around an area that is strange to them. I also have one mother available in the dressing room or backstage with needle, thread, hooks, and eyes and other notions in case of an unexpected problem.

It is a good idea to have on hand several extra headdresses, arm accessories, or unusual props that you may be using for a particular number. This prevents little tears flowing like tropical rain when some child arrives for the show and finds that she has left her cuff, gauntlet, or umbrella at home.

For any performance, whether it be for a workshop, school, or PTA program, the teacher needs dependable help on hand to produce the smoothness of a good show. This help usually comes from mothers or friends, and each person should be briefed thoroughly beforehand so he or she knows exactly what responsibilities the teacher wishes the individual to take.

Whenever possible I insist that the students be able to practice at least one time on the stage or area where we will be performing. This familiarizes them with their spacing and stage exits and entrances. By becoming familiar with the area they have a definite confidence on the night of the performance. Whenever it is impossible to use the area before performance, the teacher should visit the spot and inform the students beforehand whether they will be entering stage right or left, the approximate space of the dancing area and obstacles that might be in the way, and how much footage is available for the performance. Many times one can block off the studio room to almost the exact size of the performing area. I find that by putting these standard measures into effect at every show, whether small or large, I am saved much frustration and worry, and many gray hairs.

The big recital is the program of the year for the dance student and teacher alike. This climaxes the term and every student looks forward to this day. The teacher also anticipates the big recital, because this is when she proudly demonstrates what she has accomplished with her students through the term. All concerned look forward to this recital with unabashed pride and nervous enthusiasm.

Needless to say, the yearly recital takes much planning on the part of the teacher and much practice on the part of the student if it is to be successful. A teacher should teach toward her recital throughout the year, thus eliminating the helter-skelter havoc of trying to teach dances and skits a few weeks prior to recital time.

A good recital must have a theme. This makes it much easier to work in dance numbers and maintains continuity throughout the show.

One fact I cannot stress strongly enough to teacher, parent, and student is this—keep in mind that the student is not a professional. Dances should not be too long or too difficult. The program should keep moving with a limited number of announcements and pauses in order to keep a happy audience. Every student should perform at the recital regardless of talent or ability. Numbers should be designed in such a manner that the child's knowledge is shown in its best light. Don't make your show too long. If this should happen all dancers begin to look alike to your audience. Remember that your students have not studied long enough to be able to hold an audience spellbound for several hours.

If you have a large school and find that, in order to work all students into your program, the show is going to run over an hour and fifteen minutes then by all means have an intermission in the middle of the program. This can be planned at a time when it is necessary to change the backdrop or scenery, thus giving you an opportunity to do this and giving the audience a chance to stretch their legs, have a cigarette, or chat with one another for ten or fifteen minutes.

Speaking of scenery and backdrops, keep your changes at a minimum. Nothing bogs down a show more than long delays while curtains are drawn and scenery is being changed. Just as too much announcing or talking between numbers becomes monotonous to the audience, so does too much repetition of identical steps. When working with children, there is a limited area of accomplishment, and many times a great majority of your students are at the same work level. In order to eliminate the appearance of sameness, rely on the use of novelty numbers. These always make a welcome break in any show.

A teacher must plan all dances to be presented at the recital. She also must decide upon costuming and make sure that the costumes will be ready on time for the rehearsals. At least one dress rehearsal should be held in the auditorium where the show will be given. This allows one to experiment with lighting, time the show, and make any changes that might be necessary. It is also at this dress rehearsal that I allow parents to take their pictures. The bright lights of the movie camera and the quick bright glare of the flash bulbs can be quite irritating and distracting to the dancers on the night of the performance.

A teacher must also plan on having programs printed and on having backstage help, ushers for the audience, a dependable person in charge of lighting, and someone who can take care of all the musical equipment, such as a tape recorder, records, phonograph, or piano, etc. It is impossible to run the show alone, and although it is the teacher's and students' show, the unsung heroes who provide assistance on all the aforementioned details make it the successful production desired by all.

All persons assisting with the show should be thoroughly briefed and know their jobs. There should be parents or friends assisting in the dressing rooms, others lining the children up prior to their numbers, still others seeing to it that all students get back to the dressing rooms and into new costumes if necessary. The experienced teacher assigns all these important jobs to others so that she is free to take care of any emergency that only she can handle. Comforting a nervous child, reviewing a step combination that the entire class has suddenly forgotten, checking the volume of the music, and signaling the person on lights for a color change, are examples of the dozens of unscheduled and unplanned crises the teacher must handle herself.

Tiny tot numbers are show stealers. Be sure and include several of these in your program. The sincere effort of these little terpsichoreans cannot be equaled. It is a very rare occasion when the routine goes off as planned. Invariably some distraction or memory failure causes the tiny tots to forget their routine or repeat a few heel drops that are completely unscheduled; they might even spot a parent or relative in the audience and start a bit of conversation with them. Do not let it worry you. Just the fact that they are performing and there is some type of pattern to what they are doing is enough to give your audience tremendous enjoyment.

Good music is a must for any program and especially so for the big recital. If one is using records, be sure that they are comparatively new and not the worn and scratched records that have been played over and over again while the students have been learning and practicing their numbers. If tapes are used, be sure that they are well recorded and are played at a proper volume. If a pianist is used, have the piano situated in a place where she can see the dancers in order to keep pace should something unexpected occur during the routine.

The selection of your music is all important. Nice arrangements, played by good musicians, with excellent orchestrations and familiar melodies, not only please your audience but also lift your dancers to new heights of performance.

The ingredients, therefore, that make a good recital are a clever theme; original choreography; good music at a pleasing volume; smart costuming; short, interesting dances, sprinkled with a bit of novelty; and thorough planning. This combination gives the teacher confidence in the show and this feeling of confidence is felt by the student, who in turn gives her best performance. Also, praise and acknowledgment of jobs well done by students and helpers are not only a gesture in good manners, but help to create a feeling of fellowship.

There are any number of recital themes which one can use. Usually a teacher originates her own. She knows the ability and knowledge of her students. She sets her theme considering these two factors and works her dance routines in accordingly.

For those of you who are novices in the field and find that at this stage your creativity simply will not function when it comes to a recital theme, I will list a few. You might want to use them in the beginning, but as you become more experienced you will find that you are much happier creating your own themes.

A FOREIGN AFFAIR: The theme of this show is a tour of foreign countries, and it is one theme which requires little backdrop decoration and not too many stage settings. In fact, for this theme, a sketch of a huge ocean liner or various posters of foreign countries borrowed from a local travel agency, may be all you need.

The script should be short and witty, and I have often found that dialogue in poetic form is more interesting to use than just conversational speaking. To start, a student might board the liner in New York, inviting the audience to join her on a trip around the world. The possibilities of dance numbers which could be included in this show are unlimited. In New York, for instance, you can have jump-rope dancers performing to "The Sidewalks of New York." France naturally offers the can-can chorus, showgirl-type routines, and adagio. Ireland suggests the Irish Jig, and military numbers can be developed for many countries. Hawaiians, Japanese, and Chinese can have accessories such as fans, umbrellas, and sarongs with leis. As long as costuming typifies the country and the music blends in with the country, costume, and dance, you can use almost any type of dancing.

I have used this particular theme on many occasions and it is easy to arrange and inexpensive to produce because of the simple stage settings.

THIS IS YOUR LIFE: This is a clever theme where, in imitation of the television show, you choose a grandmotherly and grandfatherly couple out of the audience and take them through their life in a dance review. The theme requires few props and can be very entertaining. You can trace a life musically with such numbers as "You Must Have Been a Beautiful Baby," "Take Me Out to the Ball Game," and "When Paw Was Courting Maw." Add a wedding scene, military numbers for World War I, gay Paree, back to the farm, and a few grandchildren, and finish off with the sponsor offering the chosen couple a trip to the moon. Of course, the trip is done in dance form, using appropriate costumes. Once we blasted a rocket off the stage; however, this took some doing and I would not advise it for the novice teacher.

43. Stage suggestion.

THROUGHOUT THE YEAR IN DANCE: This is another theme which requires very little expense in background props. Of course, the theme itself defines the type of costuming which will be needed. January offers "Winter Wonderland" and "Let It Snow," etc. February has Valentine's Day along with Washington's and Lincoln's birthdays. March is known for its winds, and has St. Patrick's Day. April has much to offer—spring, April showers, or rains where umbrellas could be used. May is the end of the school year and also the beginning of summer, and here many flowers could be used. June has ball games, picnics, and vacations, and "June Is Busting Out All Over" could be used. Naturally, the Fourth of July will require military numbers and patriotic routines, while August offers "By the Sea," "Summertime," and a host of other songs. September brings back-to-school days, and rhythm could be included with "My Nursery Rhymes," while October can be beautiful with colorful lighting showing leaves, fall, and Indian summer. November offers Thanksgiving, sleigh rides, and trips to grandparents' farm, while December could be worked completely around Christmas. This is another easy theme that can absorb any number of students in a variety of dances.

RHYTHM REVIEW: This can be a presentation starting with beginning students and working the show right through the intermediate and into the advanced. This gives your audience some conception of the progress that students make while studying tap dancing, and the stage setting can again be set upon the backdrop, eliminating the need for scenery and scenery changes.

One of my favorite programs was when we did "Night Beat On the Ginza." We were in Tokyo at the time and this particular theme suited the occasion. We included shoppers, foreign tourists, Japanese dancers, military personnel; children on roller skates, using jump ropes, umbrellas, or fans were used for novelty numbers. You might want to do this theme using a setting in your immediate area.

A very catchy title and a very clever show was one I did in Europe called "Gershwin, By George!" In this presentation we chose all the George Gershwin melodies to use as our background music. By spending a little time on research, I was able to include on the program the date that each number was written. This was most interesting to our audience. The music was lovely, the costumes beautiful, and the expense for staging at a minimum.

A circus theme is always popular, and here one can include clowns, animal costume numbers and, of course, the trapeze artist. One time we lowered three dancers onto the stage with our own interpretation of the trapeze. This was done by having three fathers backstage handling the pulleys. One must really practice this for there is a certain amount of danger involved. Be sure you have responsible people designing your trapeze apparatus so that all safety features are included. Also be sure that you have safety-conscious people operating the backstage pulleys and students performing who have no fear of heights.

44. Stage suggestion.

Production shows are costly and should not be attempted by the teacher in the beginning stage. Choose simple themes at first until you have gained experience in presenting shows. Production shows are lovely. They call for scenery, which can be costly; precise timing for scenery changes, so that the audience is not left for too long a period of time without some type of entertainment; and many, many rehearsals.

There are many shows that can be worked around a production theme. To mention a few, Cinderella, Rip Van Winkle, and the ever popular Snow White. The scripts for these numbers are usually written by the teacher, or a professional scriptwriter is hired. The show is the actual story of whichever childrens' favorite you choose to do, and the dance numbers are worked in to blend with the continuity of the story.

One must put one's imagination to work to decide where the flowers will dance, and to work in a forest scene to present the squirrel, bird, and animal costumes. Of course, military numbers can be used for palace guards.

The scenery for production shows can sometimes be rented from a theatrical supply house. Students enjoy helping you make scenery and it is amazing how many parents have artistic talents and are eager and willing to offer their services.

This has given you ideas for a few themes to use in your recitals. As your knowledge and experience grow you will have little difficulty in designing and creating your own recital themes. The unusual and different is always appreciated, and you and only you know the capabilities of your students. Choose your theme and choreography to show off your students' accomplishments.

10

Teaching Various Age Groups

THERE ARE many different types of dance teachers and, just as every profession has its skilled and unskilled members, so does dancing. However, the majority of teachers are very dedicated to the field of dance and the progress of their students, and have many years of training and study behind them. Some have even had professional careers, while others have served as advisors for television productions and stage shows. Many have spent a number of years studying dancing, have gone through teachers' training courses, and have then started their own studios. All of the good dance teachers have not accomplished their goal overnight.

The former professional dancer is often an excellent teacher, but usually such an individual goes through a teachers' training course before opening a studio. In this course, class planning and the students' expected progress are discussed. It also affords an opportunity for the professional dancer to review the basic breakdowns and terminology which beginning students should be trained in.

The former professional dancer will probably emphasize good class discipline, for she knows that students who pay close attention to the instructor will be able to respond quickly and correctly to directions. Also, the shows and recitals put on by students of the former professional have a great deal of style, showmanship, and polish. Therefore, a teacher who has a professional background usually has much to offer a student.

159

Equally as proficient as the former professional is the teacher who has studied dancing most of her life, and, after years of training, progresses through her teachers' training course and opens her own studio. This person is familiar with dancing from a student performer's point of view and also a teacher's point of view. She has all of her class notes and training notes to rely on and, being the product of a good studio, naturally has the necessary background to bring the best out of every student. This type of teacher also has much to offer to a student.

Fortunately in the minority in the dance profession are other teachers who can be placed in two categories. One is the would-be professional, the person who never quite reached her goal and has turned to teaching as a substitute. One might say this individual is always performing and never teaching. Since she is still wrapped up in her own desires and frustrations over a goal never accomplished, there is a lack of stability and continuity in classes, programs, and routines. Oftentimes this teacher expects too much out of the students and insists that they perform at what she considers professional standards. This naturally spoils the students' own sweet, unprofessional performances.

The dance teacher in the second category is the person who studies for a year or so at a well-organized studio, who does show signs of talent, but is too impatient to undertake the necessary years of training. This person thinks she has conquered everything in one or two terms and immediately starts her own dance studio.

Woe to the child who becomes a student in these classes. Since knowledge is very limited, instructions will be also. Correct technique and style, terminology, and body placement come with years of diligent study.

It is very wise to investigate the background of the teacher with whom your child wishes to study. The ethical teacher usually has certificates, diplomas, awards, and professional background pictures on display or in files ready for any parent to inspect. She welcomes sincere questions on the part of the parent as indicative of the parent's interest, never feels that a parent is questioning her knowledge or ability.

So do not hesitate to be fully informed of your teacher's background.

Dancing instructions are important in the development of a child's body, along with proper breathing control, coordination, good balance, and quick reflexes. Improper instructions can be very harmful in these areas. Sometimes the bad habits learned in a school where instructions are not up to standard are never corrected. Therefore, you owe it to your child to investigate the background and ability of a teacher and the policy and standards of a dance school.

In most cases dancing lessons are merely a phase in a child's life. They are part of growing up. The classes and programs will give children pleasant memories as well as good posture, coordination, poise, and confidence.

Very few students who study dancing continue on into the professional field. Those who do decide on a professional career reach their goal, not through the dancing studio, but through their own agent after many years of studying and performing. However, the dancing school phase in a child's life is very important. All children love the fun of dancing and the thrill of costumed programs. They enjoy the companionship and fellowship available through classwork. Programs are a big moment in their lives and the satisfaction of achievement when steps are mastered and routines are learned is always rewarding. The influence of the dancing teacher can be beneficial in the physical and character development of the students.

Most teachers organize their classes according to the ages and abilities of the students. One finds that there are different work levels in every age group and each one needs a different type of presentation. Through my many years of teaching all over the world I have gained a great deal of knowledge in handling various age groups and this knowledge I would like to share with you.

When working with tiny tots or preschoolers one must definitely have a pleasant class atmosphere. Classes must be fun and yet productive, and it is easy to reach the happy medium. Class time cannot be wasted with idle chatter, and the little ones must realize that you do expect progress. I suggest that each child be given his particular place to stand in the classroom the very first day of lessons. Thereafter, when it is time for class to start, every child should be in his place with tap shoes tied properly and be ready to start the day's lesson.

The span of concentration is definitely limited with this age group, so one cannot work for a prolonged period of time on one particular point. The step instructions must be simple and geared to the level of the tiny tot mind. Patience must be your best virtue, for that which is very simple can seem quite difficult to the preschooler. Oftentimes dancing class is the child's first association with group work, and this in itself calls for time to adjust.

I find that the little ones enjoy being treated as maturely as possible in the classroom and are proud to know that their class is being handled just like the older student classes. I do not believe in star charts, or gum and candy rewards for this age group. Not only does it waste class time, but it also sets a bad trend for future learning. A child should not be rewarded for behaving himself during class. This is expected of him, and if promises of stars or presents are needed to bring forth good behavior, the child is not yet ready for group work.

The tiny tot has uninhibited movements and expressions and a sincere desire to learn. By keeping the class moving from the first step to another, and back again to the first step, constantly repeating, but not prolonging any one phase, the teacher can keep the students alert and enthusiastic in the classroom.

Background music should be explained simply so that they can understand. Step terminology should be explained properly, and then broken down into phrasing which this age group can grasp. Class time should never extend over a forty-five minute period. If you set class time for an hour with this age group, the last fifteen minutes are a waste of everyone's time. The child is tired both mentally and physically, and all that has been accomplished through the first part of the class is lost in the last fifteen minutes.

Routines should be designed cleverly yet kept simple and

should always be short. It is difficult for the tiny tot to remember a long routine, not to speak of complicated combinations. A simple, welldone routine is much more desirable than a difficult one performed below standard.

I find when working with this age group that it is wise to have them repeat the terminology aloud as they are doing the step. For instance, as we do a brush-brush step we say "brush-brush step" in the beginning stage. This implants the body motion in their minds and helps considerably in the memory department.

The next age group, which I classify as my subteens, are in the beginning elementary school grades and have been subjected to classwork in school and Sunday school. Their span of concentration is longer and they are accustomed to following instructions and remembering class rules. They are also very sincere about their work and want to please. This age group respects firmness in the classroom. One can conduct disciplined and progressive classes and still maintain an atmosphere of enthusiasm and happiness.

One can move at a faster pace through subteen classes since there is no need for constant repetition. However, difficult combinations cannot be performed with perfection, so the stress is still on clever simplicity. I keep classes for this age group set at forty-five minutes. Although they are out of the tiny tot stage they still have not reached a maturity where body and mind can function at best for a prolonged period of time.

It is also wise to stress to this age group the good habit of taking proper care of equipment. They are now old enough to tie their own shoes, keep their dance equipment in order in the studio and at home, and to be more self-reliant in all respects. Again, I assign class placement and expect the student to be in place properly equipped when classes start. I do not allow gum chewing, candy eating, or conversing between students. Neither do I allow student criticism of one another. This leads to hard feelings and an unhappy class atmosphere. My subteens learn at their first lesson, that I, as teacher, will do the criticizing and they, as students, will do the learning. They also realize that studio rules must be followed, and they respect class rules and studio requirements.

When working with the next age group, the preteens, a teacher must direct their progressive abilities and attitudes in the right direction. This age group is in the upper grades of elementary school and is eagerly anticipating junior high school. They are a very sincere but most forgetful age group. They will appear at class with ribbons or straps completely out of their shoes. For the first ten minutes they will work very hard and then suggest that we all rest for another ten minutes. They must be pushed and challenged constantly in order to progress as they should. They are very sharp and intelligent, but are at that in-between age where they are too old for the simplicity of the subteen, and too young for the sophistication of the teen-ager. Their frustrations are many, and a teacher must work very hard to maintain the proper class enthusiasm and progress she desires to attain.

I do not assign class placement with this age group. They know that they should be in line and properly equipped before class starts and I allow them a certain amount of self-government regarding placement. However, when I find that the lineup is running on the best-friend basis and we are not accomplishing what we should, I quickly change placement and class continues.

Sometimes one finds in this age group that one particular child is at dance class merely because her best friend is there. There is no interest in lessons or accomplishment, and absolutely no desire to learn motivating this particular student. Of course, one cannot have this attitude from any individual in the classroom. It soon rubs off on all and then there arises a difficulty. When I discover this, I immediately discuss the problem with the student and her parents. If the attitude does not change, I ask the child to please drop out of class. It is senseless to waste the parents' money and my time on an uninterested student when there is a waiting list of students eager to learn the art of tap dancing.

Progress and advancement come quickly with the preteen group. They are better coordinated due to various school sports, and they can concentrate and remember. They can understand music count, and they are very sincere and loyal. These students must be constantly challenged, and one must certainly keep enthusiasm in class at a high peak.

Working with today's teen-agers is really refreshing. They form a highly intelligent group which is worldly wise in the arts. They demand perfection from themselves and are never completely satisfied with their completed routines, always striving to do better. Usually by the time the student has reached this age she has several years of dancing behind her. She is definitely interested even if just a beginner, for she is at class because she herself wants to be there.

Many of the ideas and combinations that this age group devises are well worth including in program routines. I have my teen-agers assist with designing their own choreography. By so doing the dance becomes a part of them and the combinations used, sometimes their own creations, are the ones they can perform with greatest skill.

I do find that many times my teen-age students have sudden changes of moods. Something they might be very elated about during one class becomes dull at the next class. I try to make them realize that any type of creativeness must be respected and appreciated, for part of an individual's heart and mind has gone into it. I also stress that we cannot expect every combination or every routine to be each individual's favorite, so we must take all steps and combinations presented in our stride and do them to the very best of our ability.

I often utilize my teen-agers as class demonstrators for my other classes. This is a great help to me and also a wonderful experience for them. A class demonstrator merely demonstrates. Never does a teacher turn the class over completely to an older student.

This age group definitely needs challenge in every class. They have a deep interest, and their desire for accomplishment is very high.

It is often rewarding for the teacher and for the students as well, to organize a highly specialized performing unit with this age group. At one time my Bet-Coette Dancers spent a summer season performing for various organizations and clubs. They were paid for their performances and each student made enough money to pay for the next year's lessons and to purchase much of their needed school clothing and equipment.

I have formed several teen-age performing groups for a summer season of shows. This takes a great deal of time, planning, and hard work from both teacher and student, but the experience and monetary gain make it very worthwhile.

The student who has serious professional aspirations and a great deal of talent should receive the proper guidance from her teacher. If the desire is there, plus the determination and the ability, then a teacher should never discourage or hold back the student. She should be allowed to perform whenever possible, for each stage appearance develops more stage presence and showmanship. Technique and style should be practiced to the point of perfection, and this student should definitely be placed in time in a professional school or put into the hands of a qualified agent when the teacher feels that she is ready to enter the professional world. Few dance students have the stamina and determination that characterize the professional dancer. Those who do have these qualifications will, on their own, reach their goal. However, a teacher, and especially a teacher with a professional background, can do much to guide the student and prepare her for the stage. But the agent is the person who takes over and secures the bookings after the teacher has molded and trained the student.

Regardless of what age group one is working with, one must certainly be enthusiastic in order to have successful classes. Progress and harmonious student-teacher relations stem from enthusiasm. It is contagious and a highly successful studio has highly enthusiastic teachers. When classes are dull and boring it is a reflection on the teacher and not the students. Combinations, excercises, routines, and steps must be presented in such a way that the student wants to learn. Keep enthusiasm high and class interest will be exceptional.

Also, regardless of what age group you are working with,

remember to send notes home with the student regarding any class change, recital practices, or future programs. Do not rely on the memory of the student. During these busy days, it is so easy for a student to forget and a note is a permanent reminder.

Of course, one finds all different types of personalities among dance students and teachers. We all have our individual characteristics and traits so that not all members of one age group can be expected to act the same. You will find that in every age group, individual problems will arise and these must be handled on an individual basis. However, if you keep your group enthusiastic, pushing when necessary, offering challenges at all times, and handling problems with patient understanding, you will have successful classes. There will be an excellent student-teacher relationship and your accomplishments and achievements with your students will be rewarding for everyone.

11

Opening
Your Own Studio

MANY THINGS must be taken into consideration when opening your own dance school. First, of course, your training is behind you and you should be qualified in all phases of tap dancing. You have done this by diligently studying this book and enrolling in a studio for classes and afterward for a teacher's training course. You definitely have a love for dancing and the patience and ability to present your knowledge at a student level. You must also have a keen desire to work with children. A certain amount of dedicated confidence should also be part of your make-up, and a cheerful optimistic attitude is really an asset.

Dance schools can be opened on a shoestring or one can invest a great deal of money to start. Personally, I feel that one should open one's school on a very limited budget, regardless of available financial resources. This way the school can pay for itself, as it is very easy to overspend and overestimate your enrollment.

Location is very important. If you can, find a place close to the schools or in an area that does not have heavy traffic. In the smaller towns many of the children walk to and from dancing school. In the cities it is wise to choose a building where there is some kind of parking space available for parents' cars. You might want to start by renting a hall or auditorium one or two days a week. This is most satisfactory for, as your enrollment is building and you are establishing yourself, you do not have a high rental overhead. Some teachers find that the family room or den in their home makes an ideal place for dance classes. If you are fortunate enough to be in an area where there is no zoning, this works out satisfactorily. I have made a double garage into a most desirable dance studio and it was wonderful to be at home to teach. There should be bathroom facilities available near the studio area when teaching at home. This eliminates the necessity of all of the students having to use your family quarters for changing clothing or taking care of personal needs.

Once your location is settled your next step is advertising. Newspaper advertising would be helpful, with small spot ads running periodically after you have opened the school. When placing your newspaper advertising, inquire about the possibility of the paper running a story on the fact that you are starting a dancing school. The story should include your background and also your plans for the future. A picture of you in the story or with the ad is a very good idea. The ad should include the location of your school, when classes will start, and the dates and times of registration, along with the all important telephone numbers.

One can also advertise on radio, television, at drive-in movies, or on billboards. Whatever type of advertising you choose, try to keep costs at a minimum. In all probability you will as quickly enroll many students with small ads in the newspaper as you would with expensive ads using many inches of space.

Do not expect the calls to come in immediately or in great volume. It takes a while to establish yourself, and the very best advertising you can ever have is one satisfied student recruiting another interested student.

Plan your classes by ability and age group. I am a firm believer in classwork and do not recommend individual lessons unless the child is far behind the rest of the students her age. If so, a few individual lessons will allow the student to catch up with the rest of the group and go back into class where competition and group work are much more challenging than learning alone.

Your class schedules should usually be planned around

your area's youth activities. Saturday classes are desired by many parents and usually a teacher can teach all day on Saturday. However, there are students who do not wish to tie up a weekend with Saturday classes, so it is wise to also have some weekday classes. Keep in mind that these classes must start after school and cannot end too late in the evening, for parents frown on their children neglecting homework for dancing class.

You only have a limited amount of teaching hours during the week, of course, but if class enrollment is good it is worthwhile to absorb all interested students.

The tiny tot classes can always be scheduled in the morning or just prior to lunch. This is the time when these children are at their best. It is before nap time, and they are fresh and alert in the morning. If for some reason you cannot take a morning group of little ones, then schedule them at a practical afternoon time. Remember if these children are accustomed to taking a nap at two o'clock in the afternoon, they will not be alert through a dance class scheduled at this time.

Wherever you are teaching, it would be wise to have some type of bulletin board. This will save you much time in repeating things over and over to each class. Any bit of information that you want your students to have should be posted, and the students instructed to always read the bulletin board before coming into the classroom.

Written explanations of steps and combinations should be put on the bulletin board so that the student can copy the combination down in her class notebook before entering the classroom. If a pair of tap shoes has been misplaced, this should be announced on the bulletin board for all students to see, eliminating the need to repeat the statement in each class and thus saving valuable class time.

I insist that all students from the subteen group up have a class notebook. In this they should write down all steps, combinations, terms, and routines. This information, of course, is all put on the bulletin board and the students copy it from there. The notebook is a wonderful reference for the student. Should she forget some phase of work between classes all she has to do is refer to her class notes.

Along with the bulletin board, individual notes are very important. As I mentioned before, any bit of information that must get to the parents should be sent home as a note via the student. Granted it does take time to type or write the notes, but it is necessary in order to be certain the information gets to the right place at the right time.

Advance notice on all planned special activities is also a must. You will find that you must plan activities well ahead of time and at the earliest date notify the parents, via notes, what activity is planned, the date, the time, the place, and what necessary equipment will have to be on hand for the student. Make your notes short and concise, but be sure to include all needed information.

You will find that it is very beneficial to you to cooperate fully with your community and your community's youth programs. This not only helps to advertise your studio, it usually involves your students in programs, where they gain experience and where the public is made aware of your talent and abilities as a dance teacher.

There are many things one can do to create good community relations. Planned pageants or beauty contests can often use the help of a dancing teacher. Volunteer your studio and your services. Little theater groups may need some help with choreography from time to time. Don't hestitate to let them know that you would be delighted to assist. You gain some knowledge and experience with each venture, and the fact that you are willing to help certainly makes for good community relations.

You must make your studio rules and stand firmly behind them. These rules depend solely on what you want and expect from your students. A list of the studio rules should be given to each student when she enrolls in class, and she should be told to read them carefully since they will be enforced strictly.

Should any question arise over one of your rules, explain it clearly to the student or parent. It is important that they understand *why* you feel it is necessary to enforce the said rule.

Usually studio rules include what you do and do not allow

in the classroom, your stand on tardiness, and the required apparel. You may want to include your feelings on parents watching classes and, of course, this depends on the individual teacher. Some teachers have no objection to parents watching every class, while others wish to limit this practice to once a month or so.

You certainly should run your studio as a business, and handle books and files with care and efficiency. To most dance teachers this is a distasteful job, for their interest is in art and creativity and not in cold facts and figures. Some teachers hire an accountant, perhaps giving this person's child dance lessons in exchange for services. Other teachers hire a receptionist-bookkeeper and still others handle all business details themselves. Whatever method you choose, be sure it is an efficient one, for when income-tax time comes around, careful records of costs and expenses along with receipts of income will help your accountant prepare a proper file for you.

There should be a file card for every student, which includes name, telephone, address, father's and mother's places of business, and telephone numbers of same, doctor's name, address and telephone number, and the child's birthdate. My studio always has two card files. One file has the above information in it and the other is a birthday file. The first file is kept alphabetically while the birthday file is kept by date. It takes me just a moment at the beginning of each week to see who will be recipients of birthday cards from the studio for that week, for under the date is the child's name and address. Cards are a thoughtful gesture and greatly appreciated by each student.

To stimulate class interest one should have achievement awards or certificates. These should be presented to the student at the end-of-term recital, or at the end-of-term party given by your studio.

I use a testing program to decide which students should receive the awards. Each class is given an examination which I have previously prepared based on the work level of the particular class. All materials covered from the first lesson to the last lesson are included in the examination.

Sometimes I invite other teachers or dancers to come to the studio and grade my students on these exams. We strongly stress students' immediate recognition of the terminology along with her technique and style in executing a step or combination. They are not long exams and the students receiving the highest grades naturally receive the achievement awards.

This type of examination is also a double check on you as teacher. If one entire class does badly on one particular step, or does not even recognize the terminology and cannot remember the proper execution, you immediately realize that you, the teacher, have not stressed this particular combination enough. I do think you will benefit from such a testing system.

Your yearly recitals should be planned no later than January and materials for costumes should be ordered much in advance. I find that by using the Christmas holiday break to advantage I can come to class in January with the recital all planned and the dance routines typed and ready to be handed to each student. Do give the student a typewritten copy of the planned dance routines utilizing steps she has already learned. She can understand the terminology and is familiar with feet, body, and arm placement. The only thing you must do is to get her to perform the dance perfectly to the music. Thus, one can work on the recital dances, which include steps already learned, at the same time that the student continues to progress into more advanced work learning new steps which will be included in the next recital. As you can see, it takes constant planning ahead in order to function successfully.

A teacher must also work closely and harmoniously with parents. A good teacher-parent relationship is always desirable and takes understanding on both parts. The majority of parents are most cooperative and willing to abide by any rule or suggestion the teacher might make. In fact many of the parents offer help when it comes to transporting groups to performances. They are also life-savers when it comes to backstage help or making props and scenery.

In the minority are the stage-struck mother or the pushy

mother, but every dance teacher has had her experiences with this type of parent. The stage-struck mother insists that her child is star material, and if you do not recognize this you are not worthy of your tap shoes.

The pushy parent is going to force her little one on you, like it or not, and insists that her child is the most intelligent student you have ever enrolled. If you do not recognize this fact you are constantly enlightened by the mother, and this can tend to be very annoying after awhile.

Every teacher must handle these situations as she herself chooses. I try to appease for awhile, but if things get too far out of hand, which they usually do, I suggest the child be placed in some other school. One cannot hurt the feelings of all other students because of one demanding mother, and if this situation is not corrected immediately, studio morale drops like a falling thermometer.

You will find that as you gain knowledge through experience you will adopt your own format for classes. However I feel that the information in this chapter and throughout this book will help to guide you until you formulate your own individual approach and presentation through all phases of the tap-dancing field.

Appendix

Further information regarding all kinds of theatrical goods such as costumes, costume materials, and accessories, as well as excellent yearly catalogues may be obtained by writing to the following supply houses:

Capezio
5623 West Sunset
Los Angeles, Calif. 90028

Dance Magazine
268 West 47th St.
New York, N.Y. 10036

Dazians
318 S. Robertson
Los Angeles, Calif. 90048

Fujikake Theatrical Supply
1–21 Kotobuki
Taito-ku
Tokyo 111, Japan

Hollywood Dance Wear
6512 Van Nuys Blvd.
Van Nuys, Calif. 91401

Kent School of Dance
Bonnie Kent, Director
416 West Yakima Ave.
Yakima, Washington 98901

Leff and Jason
Theatrical Materials
51 Middlesex St.
London E 1, England

Maharam
1113 South Los Angeles St.
Los Angeles, Calif. 90015

National Association of Dancers and Artists
1920 West 3rd
Los Angeles, Calif. 90057

Pasadena Dancers Supply
464 E. Colorado
Pasadena, Calif. 91101

Rowan and Reid School of Dance
Fredericka Reid Mohr, Director
711 South Victory Blvd.
Burbank, Calif. 91502

Russell Records
Ventura, Calif. 93001

Southern Exporters and Importers
1809 Louisiana St.
Houston, Texas 77002

Style Queen Inc.
1536 7th St.
Los Angeles, Calif. 90017

Wolff and Fording Theatrical Supplies
46 Stuart St.
Boston, Mass. 02216

Index

177